FISHEATING CREEK

PRESERVING A SPECIAL PLACE IN FLORIDA'S FINAL FRONTIER

BRUCE FORD

ISBN-13: 978-1495985898

First printing March 2014

Create Space Publishing

Contact me at ford654789@comcast.net

Dedicated to:

Alexander Preston Ford Jr.
January 29, 1922 to August 23, 2010

Who took the time to take my brother Randall and me to Fisheating Creek over forty years ago, and many times thereafter.

Randall Gregory Ford
November 10, 1954 to December 9, 2013

With whom I shared a lifetime of outdoor adventures and memories, including many trips to Fisheating Creek that I will always cherish.

My wonderful wife Laurie who encouraged me to complete this book with her usual enthusiasm, positive attitude and kind words.

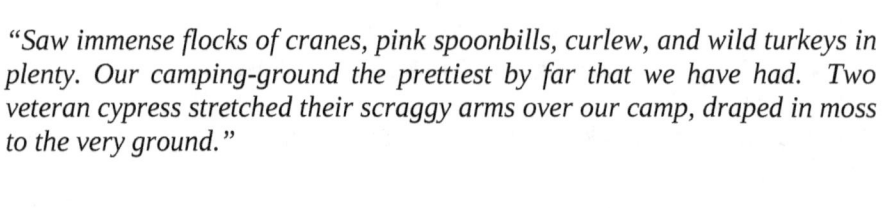

"Saw immense flocks of cranes, pink spoonbills, curlew, and wild turkeys in plenty. Our camping-ground the prettiest by far that we have had. Two veteran cypress stretched their scraggy arms over our camp, draped in moss to the very ground."

Description of Fisheating Creek upstream from Cowbone Marsh from: "A Canoe Expedition into the Everglades – 1842", George Preble, U.S. Navy.

TABLE OF CONTENTS

LIST OF PHOTO'S

INTRODUCTION

Fisheating Creek is an uncommonly beautiful blackwater creek located in the prairie country of south Central Florida. The name of the creek was derived from the Seminole Indians who referred to it as Thlothlopopkahatchee or *"The Creek Where Fish Are Eaten."* The creek meanders for 55 miles through southern Highlands County and eastern Glades County where the climate is considered sub-tropical. Of all the inflows to Lake Okeechobee, including canals, rivers and creeks, Fisheating Creek is the only one whose water flow is not controlled by a major water control structure, at least not yet. The creek's marshy headwaters are located in southern Highlands County northwest of Lake Placid where about half of the creek is located and where it has been partially altered through ditching and channelization for agriculture uses. The other half of the creek within Glades County is still in a relatively pristine condition consisting of a forested creek bottom flowing across the vast dry prairies before discharging into the marshes on the west side of Lake Okeechobee.

Florida dry prairie is an ecosystem unique to peninsular Florida which occurs from south of Orlando to north of the Everglades. Some researchers believe that the amount of dry prairie existing in pre-settlement Florida was as much as two million acres or more. Researchers believe that today only about 19 percent of the original dry prairie remains, covering approximately 385,000 acres. Dry prairie can be found on State land or on private preserves such as Kissimmee Prairie State Preserve, Avon Park Bombing Range, Three Lakes Wildlife Management Area, or the Audubon Society's Kissimmee Prairie Sanctuary. But most remaining prairie is found on the large privately owned cattle ranches in Central Florida, many of which have been in operation since the early 1800's, and have been passed down from generation to generation.

This region of Central Florida has recently been referred to as Florida's Final Frontier because it is one of the last large regions in the state not yet impacted by the urban sprawl of Florida's massive growth machine. Many of these ranches still contain significant habitats supporting numerous species of threatened and endangered animals.

Looking at NASA's "Night Lights" satellite image of the United States, you can clearly see the large dark area in the interior of Central Florida from south of Orlando all the way to the tip of the state with Lake Okeechobee in the middle. The Final Frontier covers the northern two thirds of this mostly undeveloped area and the Big Cypress Swamp and the Everglades cover the

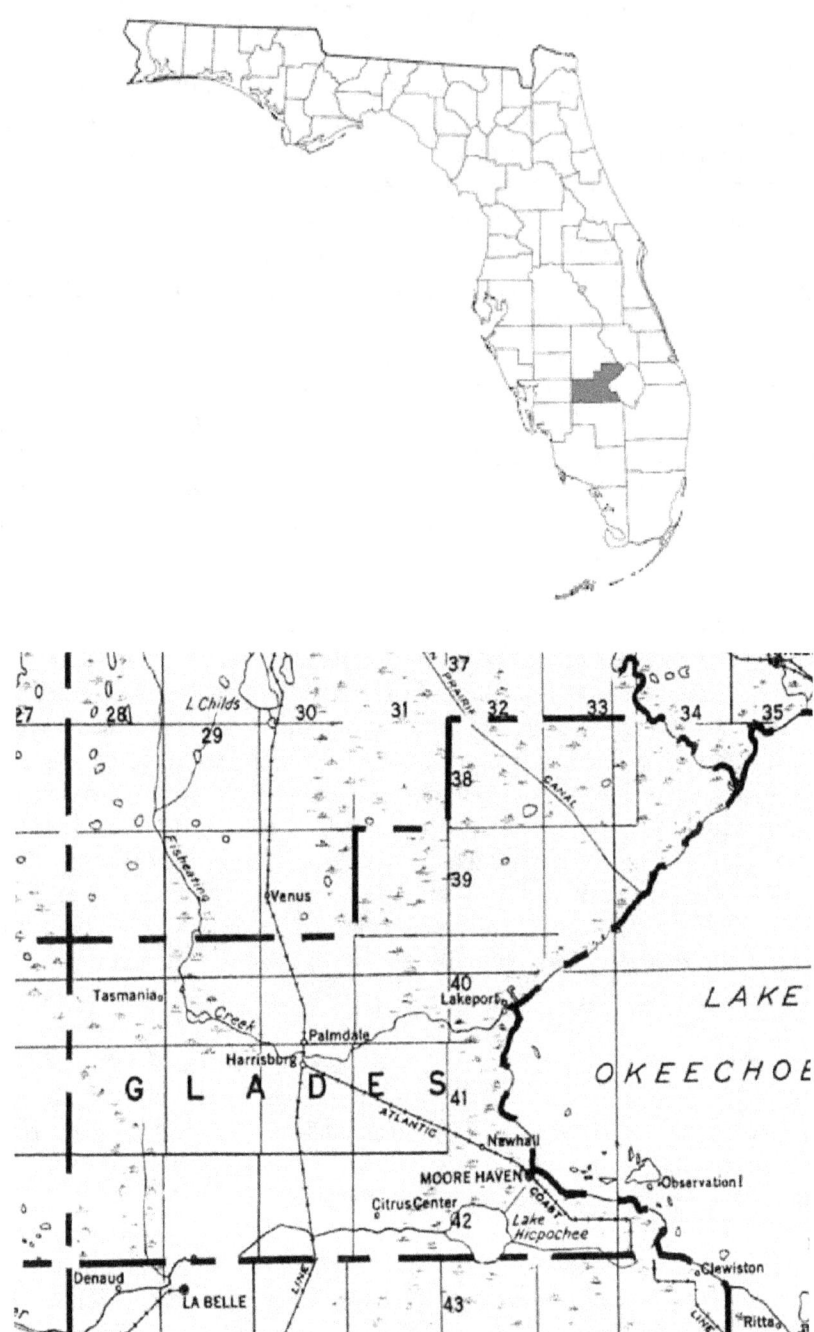

Glades County and the Fisheating Creek Region

remaining southern third of the area. The NASA image reveals that most of the remainder of peninsular Florida, especially the Atlantic and Gulf Coasts and the Orlando to Tampa megalopolis, is developed and highly populated as evidenced by the bright glow of lights. I can't think of a more compelling image than this to demonstrate the stark contrast between urban peninsular Florida and The Final Frontier.

The Fisheating Creek ecosystem is located about two thirds of the way down the Final Frontier, west of Lake Okeechobee. The majority of lands adjacent to Fisheating Creek have been owned by Lykes Brothers Corporation (Lykes) since the early 1900's and they have been managed primarily as cow/calf operations. As a result, land uses have remained low intensity and have been compatible with the habitat needs of many rare and endangered animal species found there as well as large populations of game species including white-tailed deer, wild hog, wild turkey, and bobwhite quail.

The Florida Fish and Wildlife Conservation Commission (FWC) has described the Fisheating Creek region as being strategically located between Lake Okeechobee and the Lake Wales Ridge to the east, the State owned Babcock Webb Wildlife Management Area and Babcock Ranch to the west, and the State-owned Okaloacoochee Slough and Big Cypress Swamp to the south. FWC goes on to say that this strategic location makes Fisheating Creek important to the long-term welfare of the Florida panther, Florida black bear, swallow-tailed kite, whooping crane and Florida sandhill crane, Audubon's crested caracara and a number of other species native to the region. Regarding the scenic beauty of Fisheating Creek the FWC states that *"The shaded, winding, Fisheating Creek corridor, with its black water, bald cypress swamps, hardwood hammocks and other attendant vegetation, represents an outstanding native landscape - one that has become uncommon in this part of the State."*

Significantly, the FWC has also determined that 89% of the Fisheating Creek area is a designated Strategic Habitat Conservation Area (SHCA) for one or more listed species of animals (listed as species of special concern, threatened, or endangered). SHCA's are defined as those lands which are essential to providing some of the state's rarest animals, plants, and natural communities with the land base necessary to sustain populations into the future. Despite all of the growth in Florida, the Fisheating Creek area is one of those rare places in Florida that have managed to remain relatively unspoiled and have retained some of its "Old Florida" character.

On February 19, 1998 after tens years of debate and lawsuits regarding

3

ownership of the creek bottom, Circuit Judge Charles Carlton ruled that Fisheating Creek and its adjacent floodplains within Glades County up to and including the ordinary high water line were sovereign lands belonging to the people of Florida, and not to Lykes. Lykes prepared to file an appeal, however, in order to prevent costly and time consuming litigation, the parties entered a Settlement Agreement on May 25, 1999.

The Settlement Agreement ended a long standing ownership dispute that started in 1988 between Lykes, the State of Florida, the U.S. Army Corps of Engineers, as well as two private environmental groups, Save Our Creeks Inc. and The Environmental Confederation of Southwest Florida. The ruling resulted in State fee simple ownership of the entire forty five mile long Fisheating Creek corridor within Glades County containing approximately 18,272 acres to be preserved in perpetuity.

Also in 1999, just prior to the Settlement Agreement, the Fisheating Creek Ecosystem Florida Forever project in Glades and Highlands Counties was officially added to the Florida Forever land acquisition list through sponsorship by The Nature Conservancy. Today the total project size is 176,876 acres which includes the 18,272 acres obtained from Lykes through fee simple ownership by the State per the Settlement Agreement as well as a 41,638 acre conservation easement purchased from Lykes by the State.

In addition, the State acquired a conservation easement on the 8,400 acre Smoak Groves, aka Venus Ranch, in southern Highlands County and owned by the Smoak Family. Smoak Groves was another Nature Conservancy sponsored project. The remaining acreage sought for acquisition within the Fisheating Creek Ecosystem project contains 116,966 acres, all owned by Lykes. The Florida Natural Areas Inventory (FNAI) identifies 27 rare species of plants and animals within the Fisheating Creek Ecosystem project area including two large mammals, the Florida panther (endangered) and the Florida black bear (threatened).

Unfortunately, in Central Florida, as elsewhere in the State, the coastal areas are approaching buildout, consequently, development pressures are beginning to push inland from both coasts and south from the Orlando metropolitan area towards these remaining cattle ranches in the Final Frontier including the Fisheating Creek region. Just 50 miles to the east of Fisheating Creek as the crow flies, lies the northern end of the South Florida megalopolis referred to as "The Gold Coast" where in 2014 almost 6 million people, almost a third of the State's population, are crowded into the Atlantic Coast counties of Palm Beach, Broward and Miami-Dade. Less than half that distance to the west, lie the Gulf Coast counties of Charlotte,

Lee and Collier which have a combined 2014 population of over a million persons. Florida's population in 2014 is just over 19.5 million persons and based on historical growth patterns, demographers project a 2060 population of 36 million or almost double the 2014 population. This growth will be accommodated by a projected loss of 7 million acres of undeveloped lands by 2060 including 2.7 million acres of agricultural lands and one million acres of native Florida habitat.

Growth pressures are already beginning to be felt in Glades and southern Highlands Counties. In 2007, the Florida Public Service Commission denied a Florida Power and Light Company (FPL) petition for a Determination of Need to build a 1,960 megawatt coal fired power plant on 4,900 acres of land northwest of Moore Haven. The land is owned by Lykes who would have sold it to FPL had the power plant been approved. The power plant and its 500 foot smokestack would have been located adjacent to Nicodemus Slough and just a few miles from Fisheating Creek and the world class Swallowtail kite roost site south of Cowbone Marsh.

In 2008, a Pre-Application Conference was held in Highlands County for the proposed Westby Ranch Development of Regional Impact (DRI). This DRI was proposed to be developed on 11,219 acres of the Westby Ranch located north of S.R. 70 and west of Lake Placid and bordered on the west by Fisheating Creek and its associated headwater wetlands. At buildout the mixed use project would contain up to 16,003 residential dwelling units and 800,000 gross square feet of retail along with a 175 acre Town Center. Because the project was so large, the applicant proposed it be approved as a Master Incremental DRI which would be phased out incrementally over a 40 year period from 2009 through 2049 in ten phases. The first phase was to run from 2009 through 2013 and proposed 1,700 dwelling units and 200,000 square feet of retail.

Listed species of animals observed on the Westby site include the Southern bald eagle, Southeastern American kestral, Florida sandhill crane, Audubon's crested caracara, white ibis, gopher tortoise and a Florida scrub jay was heard but not observed on the site. No information was given on how wastewater effluent and stormwater runoff were to be treated and discharged but the impacts to Fisheating Creek's water quality would no doubt be problematic. The expected DRI Application for Development Approval was never submitted and the status of this project is unclear. It should be noted that this site is now located outside Highlands County's proposed Urban Growth Area as identified on the adopted Future Land Use Map Series.

In 2009, the Highlands County Board of County Commissioners unanimously denied a rezoning request for the Eagle National Security Training Center to be located on 12 square miles of former citrus land in southwest Highlands County bordering Glades County and northwest of the small unincorporated Glades County community of Venus. This would have been a massive training facility with a one mile long runway and a 2,000 acre live fire area. The south end of the parcel would have been partially within the headwaters of Rainey Slough and John Henry Slough, both ultimately flowing into Fisheating Creek and partially within the headwaters of Gannett Slough flowing into the Peace River.

In 2012 the Florida Department of Community Affairs (DCA), the State's Chief Land Planning Agency responsible for enforcing the Growth Management Act, approved a request for a Comprehensive Plan Amendment for Blue Head Ranch, a 65,000 acre working ranch located in southwest Highlands County within the headwaters of Fisheating Creek. The owners of this ranch were successful in seeking an amendment to the Highlands County Future Land Use Map Amendment for a new designation of "Blue Head Ranch Sustainable Community Overlay" in order to develop a mixed use community which will allow up to 54,600 dwelling units, 2.5 million square feet of retail, 877,000 square feet of office, 550,000 square feet of industrial, 900 hotel rooms, and 508 acres of government, education and civic uses. The ranch had originally proposed applying for the Rural Lands Stewardship (RLS) program but then withdrew the application. Among DCA's concerns were the potential impacts to Fisheating Creek's water quality. This project is located far from Highlands County's proposed Urban Growth Area hence the need for the overlay designation. Lykes has stated that it is open to the prospect of economic development on its lands in both Glades and Highlands County.

And finally, a limited access toll road referred to as the Heartland Parkway which would run from I-4 in Polk County to eastern Lee County has been proposed by a group of large land owners collectively known as "HEART", or Heartland Economic and Agricultural Rural Task Force. The road's study corridor traverses western Glades Counties a few miles west of Fisheating Creek on land owned by Lykes and is partially within the drainage area of Rainey Slough. The proposed road also goes through the land slated to be developed for Bluehead Ranch. The Heartland Parkway has been endorsed by the Glades, Highlands and Desoto County Commissions but when former Governor Charlie Crist was in office he called it "The Road To Nowhere" and said he would not endorse it. The Florida Turnpike Authority had stated that the road as currently proposed was not economically feasible and it was on the on the back burner until

Governor Rick Scott became Governor. Unfortunately, his support along with many members of the Republican controlled legislature resulted in approval of funding in 2012 for design of a portion of the project. If built, the road would undoubtedly open up a large part of the Final Frontier to speculative development.

Perhaps because of its isolated location in the as yet sparsely developed interior of south Central Florida, Fisheating Creek has remained relatively unknown outside of South Florida. For many years canoeist, campers and nature lovers living within a two hour drive of Fisheating Creek have come from the crowded cities of southwest and southeast Florida to enjoy camping along the banks of the creek within the Fisheating Creek Campground. This campground is located in the tiny unincorporated community of Palmdale where U.S. 27 crosses the creek in Glades County.

And since the 1940's many hunters have enjoyed hunting and camping at the Fisheating Creek Wildlife Management Area (WMA). The Fisheating Creek WMA has long been known for having some of the best wild turkey hunting in the United States due to the excellent turkey habitat which the creek bottom and adjacent oak hammocks provide. This part of the State is inhabited solely by the Osceola sub-species of wild turkey which is considered by many turkey hunters to be the smartest and most difficult to hunt of all the various sub-species of wild turkey which inhabit North America.

This book describes the abundant and unique natural resources found in the Fisheating Creek Ecosystem and identifies some of the recent development pressures which have threatened it, along with some of the programs available to preserve it. It is hoped that increased awareness of this beautiful and unique area will help to preserve the remaining unprotected portions of the Fisheating Creek Ecosystem while there is still time.

2060 IS COMING

In 1959 when I was six years old, my parents moved our family from North Carolina to Orlando, Florida. Florida's population at that time was just under five million and Florida was still quite rural with agriculture being the main component of the State's economy. A drive along the Florida Turnpike west of Orlando included mile after mile of rolling hills covered in citrus and grapefruit groves as far as the eye could see and the outskirts of town were a quick trip by car where large tracts of natural lands still existed, evidence that at least part of Old Florida was still out there. The population of metropolitan Orlando in 1959 was just 335,000. Fast forward to today. In 2014, Florida's population is approaching 20 million, tourism and homebuilding are the biggest components of the economy, and Florida is the fourth (approaching third) largest State in the Union behind California, Texas and New York.

Of course Orlando's population has exploded since the opening of Disney World in 1971 and in 2014 the metropolitan population of Orlando is over two million and that population sprawls across four counties. Growth in Florida has slowed over the past few years due to the economic crisis and in fact in 2009, Florida's population actually dropped for the first time since 1946, by about 50,000 persons. However, since 1970, demographers have noted that Florida's net population has increased an average of approximately 300,000 persons per year, that's over 800 persons per day, and many demographers expect that growth rate to continue for the next thirty to fifty years. Demographers believe Florida's population in 2060 may be as high as 36 million or almost twice what it is in 2014.

With over 19.5 million people in the State in 2014, Florida is already experiencing the results of its historic high growth rates: a reduced quality of life due to among other things, crowded roads and schools, vanishing agricultural lands, and destruction of natural resources including wetlands, wildlife and groundwater.

In early 2000, the private nonprofit group, 1000 Friends of Florida, also known as the "Watchdog of Growth Management", contracted with the University of Florida's GeoPlan Center to develop a "Population Distribution Scenario for the state through the year 2060. This study included development of a series of GIS based maps to determine what Florida's land use might look like in 2020, 2040, and 2060 based on an assumption that current growth patterns would continue, no new conservation areas would be acquired, and growth rates would continue, using the Bureau of Economic and Business Research (BEBR) moderate projection of population growth.

To me, the resulting series of GeoPlan maps were disturbing to say the least and one of the key reasons I decided to write this book. The first map depicted Florida's existing urban areas in 2005 when the population was just under 18 million. Another set of maps was produced for the entire State as well as by region of Florida for 2020, 2040, and 2060. The State map for 2060 depicts the location of the urban growth areas when the population is projected to be 36 million. This map depicts peninsula Florida in 2060 from coast to coast as almost built out from Jacksonville to Miami along the Atlantic coast, from Crystal River to Naples along the Gulf coast and in the interior from Lake City south through Gainesville, Ocala, Orlando, Lakeland, and south past Sebring along the Lake Wales Ridge. A vast megalopolis with very few open areas other than existing public conservation lands.

The maps were accompanied by a summary report that concluded Florida would lose an additional 7 million acres of undeveloped lands by 2060 including 2.7 million acres of agricultural lands and one million acres of native habitat. The study also concluded that the counties to undergo the most dramatic changes based on the percentage of increase in urban areas would be Glades (the location of Fisheating Creek), Hardee, DeSoto, Hendry, Osceola, Baker, Flagler and Santa Rosa. The Fisheating Creek Ecosystem is located in the path of this projected growth. Glades County in which the Fisheating Creek Ecosystem is primarily located, was ranked first because it would have the highest percentage increase in urban area of 14.9%.

In particular the report states that the three counties which will experience the greatest transformation over the next fifty years, as they go from largely rural to largely urban, will be Desoto, Hendry and Glades. The Report states that these three Counties will receive "spillover growth" from Charlotte, Lee and Collier Counties on the Gulf Coast which they predict will be built out before 2060 as one continuous band of urban development. The GeoCenter also contracted with the Center for Quality Growth and Regional Development at the Georgia Institute of Technology to provide guidance to the State's leaders and citizens on how to deal with this growth in a more proactive manner.

Another map was subsequently produced by the University of Central Florida's Metropolitan Center for Regional Studies which depicts Florida in 2060 with the same population of 36 million but with growth directed to appropriate areas using smart growth principals that include more compact

9

urban development and less urban sprawl. The Smart Growth map looks vastly different and there is much more open space.

The Smart Growth Map gives me some hope for the future of Florida's natural resources and quality of life, however, there is reason to be skeptical because after twenty five years, Florida's Growth Management Act which was passed in 1985, has not done a very good job of preserving Florida's natural environment or maintaining the State's quality of life. Future Land Use Maps of local Comprehensive Plans are routinely amended to expand the urban boundaries, change land uses from low density agricultural uses to high density land uses, or to accommodate large DRI's with little regard of the cumulative impacts to natural environmental system. Even the best of Growth Management Plans can be, and are, derailed by local politics and/or pressure from development interests.

Since its passage, the Florida's Growth Management Act has been watered down numerous times by development interests and Tom Pelham, the former director of DCA, called it "a mess." Since its passage, hundreds of thousands of acres of citrus, cow pastures, woodlands, and wetlands have been replaced with urban sprawl. Most of Florida's coastline is built out and developers are turning to the interior of the State where undeveloped land is still plentiful and relatively cheap especially by South Florida standards. Planners who have reviewed the Growth Management Act admit that it is broken and that fixing it is imperative but there will not be any easy remedies because growth management is such a complex issue with many variables and competing interests. Pelham resigned from DCA on January 3, 2011 one day before the inauguration of Rick Scott. Governor Scott had called the DCA a job killing agency and after taking office he promptly renamed it the "Department of Economic Opportunity" or DEO. To prevent confusion, I will continue to refer to it as DCA throughout this book.

Hopefully, Smart Growth Initiatives will improve the way growth has been managed for the past 25 years. I believe, however, that the best hope for preservation of Florida's remaining natural lands, including the Fisheating Creek Ecosystem, will continue to be accomplished through land acquisition and/or conservation easements or through other voluntary incentives for landowners to preserve their lands.

Fortunately, Florida has the most progressive land acquisition program in the Nation which began in 1968 with establishment of a $20 million bond program to acquire outdoor recreation lands. That program has since evolved over the years: the 1972 Environmentally Endangered Lands Program; the 1979 Conservation and Recreational Lands Program; the 1981

Save Our Coast and Save Our Rivers Programs; the 1990 Florida Preservation 2000 program (P2000); and finally to the current 2000 Florida Forever program. The P2000 program allocated $300 million per year for land acquisition. P2000 has preserved more than 1.8 million acres of conservation lands. Florida Forever has also allocated 300 million per year and so far has preserved 638,600 acres of conservation lands and cultural resources. In addition, 29 of Florida's 67 Counties as well as eight municipalities have created land acquisition programs to purchase conservation lands.

Land acquisition by public agencies and private conservation groups has helped protect many acres of sensitive lands in Florida. However, there will never be enough money to protect all of Florida's critical lands and waters and more emphasis needs to be placed on incentive-based approaches to protect critical lands owned and managed by private individuals. This is especially important since the future of Florida Forever, the State's land acquisition program, is uncertain. Due to the economic crisis resulting from the Great Recession, including a severe reduction in home sales and property values, the State's budget has been severely strained for the past few years. As a result, for the first time since its inception in 2000, funding for Florida Forever was not approved during the 2009 legislative session. Fortunately partial funding has been approved again since 2010 but the fate of Florida Forever is still unsure at this time.

Like many Floridians who have grown up in Florida, I have witnessed the constant and rapid changes to the environment brought by the State's never ending growth. In his recently published book (2010) entitled "The Last Empty Places", author Peter Stark describes how nature writer Henry David Thoreau, author of "Walden Pond", witnessed the onslaught of the Industrial Revolution in his beloved New England during the 1840's. Stark writes that "Thoreau watched as railroad tracks were laid through his precious Concord woods and fields and along nearby Walden Pond." He states that Thoreau bought 40 acres around Walden Pond to save it from being logged and where he later built a cabin and wrote his famous book. Regarding Thoreau, Stark states that "The tide of development surged all around him. Timber fellers cut the forests nearby, and work crews arrived at Walden in winter to saw out blocks of ice for Boston's summer refrigeration. This sense of imminent threat and destruction made what remained of Wild Nature all the more precious for Thoreau."

To me this sums up perfectly what many Floridians have experienced and how they feel about growth, especially those living in the higher growth areas of the State. Those who care about the environment, their communities, and their sense of place have over the years and decades witnessed the unrelenting changes within their state and their communities. As a teenager, I first became aware of this feeling of natures impermanence and sense of loss not long after my family moved from sleepy Orlando (before Disney) to bustling Ft. Lauderdale in the summer of 1968.

At that time in Broward County, the population was less than 600,000 and it was primarily concentrated between the Atlantic coast and US 441 (aka SR 7) located approximately 7 miles west of the coast. US 441 is a major arterial running north/south between the Atlantic coast and the Everglades. The levee containing the eastern side of the remaining Everglades within Broward County was constructed in 1964 and is referred to by the South Florida Water Management District as L-36. L-36 is located approximately 6 miles west of US 441 and also runs north/south.

After construction of the L-36 levee was completed, there were still many square miles of relic Everglades habitat consisting of sawgrass marsh, tree islands, cypress strands and tropical hardwood hammocks remaining east of the L-36 levee. However, completion of the L-36 hastened the drainage and development of this remaining Everglades habitat east of the L-36 for agricultural and residential uses. Growth in Broward County has now pushed west all the way to the L-36 and the County is approaching buildout. The L-36 levee ended up serving as a de- facto urban growth boundary for Broward County.

However, in 1968, this area of Broward County between US 441 west to the L-36 and from Broward Boulevard north to the Palm Beach County line, encompassing over 80 square miles of land, was still mostly un-urbanized. This area contained agriculture, plant nurseries, pine flatwoods, cypress swamps and sawgrass marshes along with a few small cities on the perimeter that had recently incorporated in the 50's and early 60's such as Plantation, Margate and Coral Springs. Urban growth was beginning to head west towards the last undeveloped lands west of US 441 including the last remnants of the Everglades.

My late brother Randall and I loved to explore the outdoors and as soon as we could legally drive, we headed out in our 1965 Mustang to these last remnants of wildlands remaining in western Broward County to see if we could find places to hunt. One particular cool fall day in 1969 we discovered a large tract of undeveloped land bounded by US 441 on the east, levee L-36 on the west, what is now Oakland Park Boulevard on the south, and Cypress Creek Canal on the north. This tract contained between 18 and 20 square miles of mostly undeveloped wildlands and according to the local paper, a portion of it was going to be developed soon with several new golf course communities. A large portion of the tract had been referred to in the local paper as the "Behring Tract" after the name of its owner, Ken Behring who had moved to Fort Lauderdale in 1956 and shortly thereafter formed the Behring Construction Company. He purchased this tract of land for a future city to be named Tamarac. At that time, Commercial Boulevard was a dirt road west of the Florida Turnpike and we headed west on this dirt road for a couple of miles until we came to another dirt road that ran north. This road is now called University Drive. A very large and dense cypress swamp strand was located just south of this intersection oriented in an east/west fashion.

We drove north for about two miles and just before the road ended at Cypress Creek Canal there was a hunting camp on the right side of the road with a large camping tent and a half track swamp buggy along with a truck and trailer used to haul the buggy. Randall and I saw two couples at the camp and decided to stop and talk to them about the hunting. They told us they were from West Palm Beach and they had hunted deer on this land for years from their swamp buggy. They told us that this may be their last time hunting here because the land was going to be developed soon. Indeed we could see where certain areas had recently been cleared and there were piles of burning brush and trees.

The men told us that their wives had watched two large buck deer walk near the camp the previous morning while the men were out on the buggy. The men asked us if we would like to go hunting with them on their buggy so we jumped at the chance, having never been on a buggy before. The four of us got on the buggy and headed west towards the Everglades. We traveled a couple of miles and could see the L-36 off to the west less than a mile away. We then traveled south and parallel to the L-36 to the dirt road that would eventually become Commercial Boulevard. We turned to the east and headed back towards the hunting camp and saw one deer running off through the sawgrass. Close to the camp we came upon another hunter who had just killed a very large diamondback rattlesnake. The snake had recently eaten a rabbit and you could still the lump formed by the rabbit inside the snake. As the sun began to set the hunters stopped the buggy at the edge of a cypress swamp and decided to sit and watch for deer in the vicinity.

As we sat watching the sun slowly going down, we could hear hunting dogs off to the southwest baying as they trailed a deer running through the cypress swamps and sawgrass marshes. I remember the melancholy feeling I had listening to those dogs because even though I was enjoying the moment, I was also aware that this land and the wildlife that inhabited it would soon be gone as development encroached on one of the last traces of Broward County wildlands. Sure enough, as the hunters had predicted, the following year the area had started to build up and no hunting was allowed; and development was quickly changing the land from rural to urban.

Today, over forty years later, the population of Broward County has almost tripled from that in 1968 and is now approaching 1.8 million persons. For twenty years Randall and his family lived less than a mile from that dirt road intersection which has now become the very busy intersection of Commercial Boulevard and University Drive where thousands of cars and their passengers pass through it daily. The site of the hunting camp is now part of University Boulevard, a busy four lane road and that tract of land we hunted on is now home to the bustling cities of North Lauderdale, Lauderhill, and Tamarac which have a combined population of over 160,000 along with numerous golf courses including Jackie Gleason's Inverrary Country Club. A quick look at a Google satellite image shows how the entire tract of land is now urbanized. Little evidence remains of that large cypress swamp we saw in 1969.

FLORIDA'S FINAL FRONTIER

The Fisheating Creek Ecosystem is located within a unique region of Florida referred to recently as the Florida's Final Frontier. This is a region of Central Florida working ranches, wet and dry prairies, pine flatwoods, and oak and palm hammocks as well as public and private conservation lands. The region is also referred to as the Northern Everglades because it serves as a headwater area for the Everglades proper and is occupied by the Kissimmee River and Lake Okeechobee drainage basins where rainfall ultimately discharges into the Everglades.

The boundaries of The Final Frontier are not officially defined, but in general, it is the area corresponding roughly from the vast Moran-owned Deseret Ranch to the north sprawling over almost 300,000 acres between Orlando and Melbourne; the Big Cypress National Preserve and Florida panther National Wildlife Refuge on the south; the St. Johns River and Lake Okeechobee on the east; and the Kissimmee Chain of Lakes, Lake Wales Ridge, Fisheating Creek Ecosystem, Babcock Ranch, and Corkscrew Swamp on west.

Dry prairie is a dominant feature of the Final Frontier and cattle ranching and dry prairie have coexisted since the first Europeans began settling in Central Florida several hundred years ago. Historians believe the first cattle to set foot in Florida were brought over by Ponce de Leon in 1521 when he landed in Southwest Florida on his second expedition. Some of these cattle, thought to be Andalusian Heifers, escaped and became feral. Pedro Menendez also brought over cattle when he sailed to St. Augustine in 1565. Spanish Missionaries used local Indians to help tend these cattle and over time the Indians became expert cattlemen in their own right, often owning large herds.

By 1618 Spanish Governors in Florida were expanding cattle production where cattle did quite well on the vast prairies and ranges. By 1640 there was a shortage of beef and the Spanish began importing cattle to Florida from Cuba. Florida cattlemen eventually smuggled cattle back to Cuba in exchange for gold which was the beginning of commercial trade with Cuba that would last over 300 years. By 1698, cattle in Florida were located in three major areas: the St. Johns River near Palatka, Apalachee in the Tallahassee area, and in the Gainesville area.

By the early 1800's cattle had become established throughout the State, especially in the area between Orlando and the Everglades and cattle drives were commonplace. Cattle were driven from Central Florida north to markets as far away as Jacksonville, Savannah, and Charleston and to railheads in Gainesville and Baldwin, west of Jacksonville. By 1830 trade with Cuba had expanded and cattle drives from Central Florida began to go south and west to coastal ports in Tampa, Punta Gorda, Punta Rassa, and Ft. Myers for shipment to Cuba. By 1860 Florida had approximately 388,000 head of cattle and was second only to Texas in per capita value of livestock.

During the Civil War Florida was the leading supplier of beef to troops on both sides of the conflict. After the Civil War the cattle trade with Cuba for gold helped Florida weather the reconstruction period and became the foundation for Florida's vast cattle empire. Between 1868 and 1878 it is estimated that 1.6 million cattle were exported primarily to Cuba but also to the Bahamas and Key West. By 1905 trade with Cuba had decreased due to competition from Texas and South America. However, this was compensated somewhat by the fact that Florida beef was increasingly becoming an important source of beef to the southeastern U.S.

Events in the early 1920's caused a gradual change in the way cattle were raised in Central Florida. Texas Tick Fever spread throughout Florida's free ranging cattle which resulted in a Statewide program in the early 30's requiring all cattle to be inoculated every 14 days by dipping them in cement cattle vats. These constant roundups hastened fencing in of cattle and fewer free ranging cattle. Consequently, many ranchers owning smaller cattle ranches who could not afford to fence, were forced out of business.

In the mid 1930's Florida imported many starving cattle from western states impacted by the Dust Bowl. Unfortunately, some of these cattle were infected with the fly born screw worm which quickly spread throughout the Florida cattle population. Again the cattle had to be rounded up and inspected every day to prevent the spread of this disease and ranchers had to stop using catch dogs and branding since these provided opportunities for the flies to lay their eggs in skin wounds of cattle.

These events also hastened the fencing in of formally free ranging Florida cattle. Rail lines had also spread south into Central Florida providing ranchers with easy access to ports and markets as far away as Chicago. The rail lines opened up additional markets to the ranchers but also hastened the end of free ranging cattle due to conflicts with cattle crossing rail lines as well as increases in urban development which followed the rail lines south.

However, even in the 1930's it was still possible to drive cattle long distances through open range land but this tradition was soon to be a thing of the past as Florida's population continued to grow. In 1949, Florida passed a law requiring owners to fence in their livestock which effectively ended the long tradition of open range cattle ranching. Many people, even those living in Florida do not realize the current extent of the cattle industry in Florida. Florida ranks third in the number of beef brood cows east of the Mississippi River and eleventh Nationwide. Today, two thirds of Florida's cattle are found between Orlando and the Everglades on 3.9 million acres of rangeland. In 2008 there was an estimated 1.7 million head of cattle in Florida including one million beef cattle. The Church of Latter Day Saints owns one of the largest single cow/calf operations in the U.S. know as Deseret Ranch which is located on 300,000 acres (468 square miles) sprawling across three Counties (Orange, Osceola and Brevard) between Orlando and Melbourne.

Today Florida's ranch lands consist of a combination of improved pasture, unimproved or semi-native pasture, and native rangeland. Improved pasture has typically been plowed, fertilized, and limed and most often planted with Bahia grass. Unimproved or semi-native pasture is typically unplowed, unfertilized and unlimed and consist of a mix of native habitats such as dry and wet prairie, palm savannas, as well as exotic grasses. Native rangeland consist of unaltered dry prairie habitats.

Cattle ranches are an important sector of the Florida economy and in 2003 they contributed $348 million to the economy. In addition, economist point out that even though their proportion of total revenue contributed to the tax base is small compared to residential development, it is more than enough to pay for what little services they require from local governments, such as roads, fire, police, schools, etc. Previous studies on this subject have shown that for every local government tax dollar collected from agriculture, 60 cents is needed to provide services compared to $1.25 or more needed for services to residential development. In other words, residential development is subsidized by the tax payers. Studies have also shown that the most cost effective way for Counties to maintain open space and wildlife habitats is to encourage private land owners to continue low intensity agricultural practices like cattle ranching.

As urban sprawl has encroached closer and closer to these ranches, ranch lands have increased in value, and the pressure to sell to developers has increased significantly. As ranch lands have increased in value, the inheritance tax, which ranges between 45 and 55 percent, has become prohibitively high. In addition, many ranchers are at or near retirement age and their children may not be interested in working the land. So selling for development is a much more lucrative option which will allow them to enjoy their retirement years in comfort. I believe that many ranchers love their land would prefer to preserve the land for their kids and grandkids.

However, profitability is the bottom line for most ranchers in deciding whether to keep ranching or to sell. If it's profitable to keep land in agriculture, the industry will survive, but if it is more profitable to sell the land for development, the industry will suffer or outright disappear in Florida. A key point is that the economic incentives provided to ranchers by traditional conservation programs have not kept up with the escalating land values, making these incentives less attractive to land owners.

It's difficult for some ranchers to resist the temptation to sell their land to developers when the profits can be so enticing. Recent examples of this can be found throughout the Final Frontier. In 2005 in Osceola County, the Latt Maxey Corporation sold a 27,400 acre tract of citrus and ranch land in a rural area near Yeehaw Junction (between Vero Beach and Lake Wales) to a south Florida developer for an astounding $137 million during the peak of the speculative real estate boom. The FDEP wanted to buy the property for preservation but unfortunately the parcel was offered through a sealed bid process and FDEP could not come close to matching developer's high offer. The late Latimer Maxey, founder of the corporation, bought the parent tract of 100,000 acres in the early 1930's. The company is still in the ranching and citrus business but sold the land as part of a "planned asset diversification strategy."   The developer plans to build a mixed use development on the parcel, which is currently miles from any existing development, with up to 40,000 dwelling units (that's 100,000 people) as well as a town center with commercial and industrial uses, a research facility and a hospital.

In the 1950's, the Morman Church of Latter Day Saints bought 300,000 acres of Florida property sprawling across Orange, Osceola and Brevard Counties. They named the property Deseret Ranch and it has been a working ranch for over 50 years. The Ranch is a mosaic of wetlands and woodlands as well as agricultural uses including cattle, sod, citrus and timber. When I was a young boy living in Orlando in the 1960's my best friend and his family belonged to a hunt club on the ranch. It was located south of the then Beeline Highway, now know as the Martin Anderson Beachline Expressway or S.R. 528. I spent a weekend there in 1966 quail hunting with my friend and his dad and their pointer, driving through the remote pine flatwoods in their old jeep. I remember seeing large herds of deer running through those pine flatwoods. It is still a large remote and beautiful place. However, growth from the metropolitan Orlando area has slowly moved closer and closer to the Ranch over the years. In 2008, the Ranch approached Orange County officials with a plan to rezone approximately 4,578 acres of the land located in southeast Orange County, in order to develop up to 10,000 residential dwelling units. Approval would also require the County to agree to extend the existing Urban Growth boundary to the southeast to take in the proposed development site.

The Ranch subsequently withdrew their request due to questions and concerns from Orange County planners about the impacts the development would have on the surrounding region. However, the Morman Church is currently seeking approval from Osceola County and the State for amendments to the Osceola County Comprehensive Plan, including Conceptual Master Plans for several communities proposed on portions of the Ranch.

In southwest Highlands County, owners of the Blue Head Ranch, a 65,000 acre working ranch located in the headwaters of Fisheating Creek and miles from any existing development, received approval from the State for an amendment to the Highlands County Comprehensive Plan. It includes a change to the Highlands County Future Land Use Map to develop a new town to include 54,600 dwelling units, and millions of square feet of commercial, retail, industrial and civic space. The ranch had originally proposed applying for the Rural Lands Stewardship (RLS) program but then withdrew the application.

To me, one of the most disturbing examples of the pressure to sell ranch lands is the McDaniel Ranch located in southern Hendry County about an hour south of Fisheating Creek. This remote ranch is at the south end of the Final Frontier and is bounded on the south by the Big Cypress Seminole Indian Reservation and is prime Panther habitat. According to the ranch's website, the ranch was founded in the 1936 and encompasses a whopping 23,040 acres or 36 contiguous square miles in southern Hendry County. By the 1970's, the owners son had built the ranch up to 5,000 cattle. Today the ranch consists of citrus, sugarcane (which is being phased out), row crops (which are leased to independent growers), pasture as well as approximately 5,500 acres of native rangeland, oak hammocks and cypress swamps.

The ranch is home to many threatened and endangered animal species including the Florida panther, black bear, Audubon's crested caracara, swallow-tailed kite, Florida sandhill crane, Florida burrowing owl, Southern bald eagle, great egret and least bittern. In 2001 Florida Forever added a project know as Panther Glades to the 2001 Land Acquisition Priority list. Today the Panther Glades project boundary contains 64,701 acres, including about half of the McDaniel Ranch acreage located west of C.R. 833 which bisects the ranch into east and west tracts.

Unfortunately, in 2004 the McDaniel family signed an agreement to sell almost all of the ranch (20,000 acres) for approximately $95 million to a Palm Beach Gardens developer who announced plans to build a new 25,000 dwelling unit community in the wilds of south Florida. The agreement was for the developer to buy the ranch in phases over several years. He initially bought 3,200 acres in two separate parcels for almost $16 million.

Then the deal went south and the McDaniel's decided they would not sell the remaining acreage. The McDaniel family said the developer walked away from the deal and the developer said the McDaniel's did not live up to their contract. In the mean time, the developer has decided to develop the land he already bought and with a request to build 237 upscale homes on 3,041 acres. The dispute is still tied up in the Florida Courts but the developer has stated he still wants to develop the entire 20,000 acres although at a reduced scale. The ranch is not located near any development and appears to be a prime example of urban sprawl.

It's not clear, other than the prospect of lots of money, why the McDaniel's decided to sell the majority of the ranch since they had publicly stated that the ranch is part of their heritage and is their home. They stated that it's hard to make a profit in ranching and they have in fact recently spent several million dollars using their own equipment and labor to construct a massive 3,000 acre onsite water management system. The system consists of dikes, weirs, culverts, irrigation pumps, and over 44 miles of levees on the ranch to meet water quality standards requiring reduced phosphorus runoff into the Everglades.

Fortunately there has been renewed interest recently in the importance and uniqueness of Florida's Final Frontier. In April 2010 the Obama Administration announced "America's Great Outdoors" program which includes conservation of "large iconic landscapes." The Northern Everglades was given top priority in this program and it was announced that the Nature Conservancy would be working with the United States Fish and Wildlife Service (FWS) on proposals to create a new National Wildlife Refuge within the region to conserve imperiled species and habitats. According to sources who were briefed on the proposal the refuge could encompass as much as 100,000 acres. The Nature Conservancy (TNC), Florida Chapter is heading up the planning effort and is envisioning a core preserve of 25 to 50 thousand acres along with smaller satellite preserves scattered throughout the region. No lands have been purchased to date however the FWS has put the highest priority on lands located adjacent to the south end of Lake Kissimmee; land adjacent to Kissimmee Prairie State Preserve; lands just west and north of Lake Hatchineha near the Disney

Wilderness Preserve, land in the vicinity of Lake Conlin east of Kissimmee; and on lands west of Arbuckle State Park.

LYKES BROTHERS CORPORATION

The Lykes Brothers Corporation (Lykes) owns and operates what is known as the Lykes Ranch, a vast area encompassing over 350,000 acres within Glades and Highlands Counties and one of the largest ranches within the Final Frontier as well as Florida. The ranch has over 22,000 head of cattle, and is the fifth largest cow-calf operation in the United States. In addition to cattle, the ranch has diversified into citrus, forestry, sod and sugarcane operations. The ranch has the largest managed pine forest in South Florida and has developed a hybrid pine from slash pine and Caribbean pine. Lykes has also planted large stands of eucalyptus trees which are used for mulch and is now the largest grower of eucalyptus trees east of the Mississippi River. The Lykes empire began as a small family business in the 1880's when Doctor Howell Tyson Lykes left a career in medicine and began raising cattle and citrus on the family homestead in Hernando County Florida north of Tampa. By 1900, Doctor Lykes had moved his operations to Tampa and was shipping cattle to Cuba aboard a three masted schooner. By 1910 the Doctor's seven sons were also involved in the business and the family incorporated the business as Lykes Co.

In 1967 Joe Lykes, the last of the seven brothers died and over the next twenty years, Chester Ferguson, a Tampa trial lawyer who married into the family, grew the family business into a major corporation. By the late 1980's, the Lykes empire had peaked to include not only ranching and farming in Florida and Texas but also ownership of People's Gas (Lykes Energy), the states largest natural gas utility; First National Bank at Tampa (later First Florida Bank); Lykes Meat Group in Tampa; and Lykes Pasco, a large juice processing company. At one time the company also owned the worlds largest steamship line.

In the 1990's Lykes began to sell off portions of the company including First Florida Bank, Lykes Meat Group, and Lykes Energy. The proceeds from these sales were divided up between over 250 family members. In 1999 the company sold Lykes Pasco which accounted for 90% of the company's net sales and operating income and 80% of its employees. Under Florida Law, the sale of Lykes Pasco represented substantially all of the companies assets which allowed 81 dissenting shareholders opposing the sale and who held 26% of the company shares, to cash out. However, when Lykes told the investors what their shares were worth, they accused the company of low-balling them, by offering to pay them only half of what the shares had been valued just months before. As a result the shareholders, all either family members or their trustees, were forced by Lykes into court to settle the issue. The case was finally settled two years later but the amount was undisclosed. However, Lykes had offered to pay the shareholders $23 million and the shareholders wanted $103 million so the out of court offer was presumably somewhere between this range.

After the settlement, the company CEO stated that Lykes would continue to build on its existing businesses and look for new opportunities. Since then, it appears that some of these opportunities are development related including the approved Muse Village mixed use DRI development just north of LaBelle; the proposed sale of land to FPL for the now defunct Glades Power Park; the proposed Lake Placid Groves DRI currently under review by DCA which is a Mixed Use project located on 2,182 acres of existing citrus groves between Sebring and Lake Placid; competition for the proposed Inland Port sought by the Port of Palm Beach and subsequent shift to an Integrated Intermodel Logistics Center on land owned by Lykes and Duda outside of Moore Haven; and the Lykes support and backing for the landowner driven Heartland Parkway Toll Road (AKA, Road To Nowhere) which would pass through the western portion of Lykes landholding in Glades County just west of Fisheating Creek.

In addition, in 2007 Lykes sent their land manager to the Highlands County Commission meeting to publicly state Lykes opposition to the proposed Highlands County Urban Growth Boundary. Most of Lykes landholdings in Highlands County are located outside that growth boundary. And finally, in 2007 Lykes proposed a Rural Lands Stewardship (RLS) designation on its holdings in both Counties but later withdrew the request.

The RLS program is a transfer of development rights program designed to promote protection of large rural landscapes. The RLS program was added to the State Growth Management Act (GMA) in 2007, as an option for large landowners who to desire to develop their property. Development credits are determined by the value of the land to be protected also known as the sending area. These credits are then transferred or sent to the receiving area where the development is to occur. Sending and receiving areas must total at least 10,000 acres and can be in individual or multiple ownerships. RLS agreements must be approved by DCA as an amendment to the County Comprehensive Plan. Potential changes being considered by DCA to this program may include requirements for the receiving area to be located within or near existing urban areas to reduce urban sprawl and fragmentation of large rural landscapes.

Lykes has stated that even though it is no longer pursuing the RLS designation, it remains open to the prospect of economic development in both counties. At the time of the Lykes RLS proposal, Glades County stated at a County public hearing that the Lykes RLS proposal would cover 260,000 acres of Lykes land in Glades County, of which 150,000 to 200,000 acres would remain in private conservation easements and the remaining 60,000 to 110,000 acres would be developed into small towns no large than 5,000 acres each.

As noted in the Forward to this book, per the Fisheating Creek Settlement Agreement, ownership of the entire forty five mile long Fisheating Creek corridor within Glades County containing approximately 18,168 acres was transferred from Lykes to the State to be preserved in perpetuity. Also per the Settlement Agreement the State purchased 41,606 acres of conservation easements from Lykes for a total of 59,774 protected acres protected as either fee simple ownership or less than fee conservation easements.

The 1999 purchase of the creek corridor was the culmination of a long standing dispute between Lykes, who had previously asserted their ownership of the creek, and the Trustees of the Internal Improvement Trust Fund, the United States Army Corp. of Engineers (COE), Save Our Creeks Inc., and the Environmental Confederation of Southwest Florida, who asserted that the creek, up to the Ordinary High Water line belonged to the people of the State of Florida.

After almost forty years of good will and cooperation between Lykes and the State which included the FWC's longtime management of the Fisheating Creek Wildlife Management Area for public outdoor recreation, things changed in 1988. In response to concerns about illegal access to their land, Lykes blocked access to the creek by felling at least 80 trees along portions of the creek, posting "no trespassing" signs and stringing barbed wire fences and gates across the creek channel in several places. The State sued Lykes in Federal district court and asserted that the Rivers and Harbors Act prohibits obstruction of navigable waters and Lykes must remove the obstructions and allow public access. The district court dismissed the State's lawsuit and ruled that Florida must first pursue administrative remedies such as requesting the COE to perform a determination of navigability.

In 1993 the State then sued the COE to compel it to make a determination of navigability. The COE responded by undertaking a study and preparing a report which concluded that Fisheating Creek was a navigable water of the United States from its mouth at Lake Okeechobee upstream to the C.R. 731 bridge in Highlands County near the unincorporated community of Venus, Florida. The State then dropped its lawsuit against the COE. Lykes then removed all the obstructions in the creek but requested a permit from the

COE to allow Lykes to maintain fencing and operable gates at two crossings in the creek.

Lykes then sued the COE in Federal district court seeking review of the COE finding of navigability. The district court found that Fisheating Creek was only navigable to Fort Center, a few miles upstream from its mouth. The court's determination was based on a finding that Cowbone Marsh, a few miles upstream of Fort Center "has been a non-navigable marsh for hundreds of years, without any defined or navigable channel."

The COE and the State then appealed the district court's decision in the 11th Circuit Court of Appeals based on two issues. One was whether the court's factual findings were erroneous and second was whether the court applied the appropriate legal standard to its finding of navigability. Under the Rivers and Harbors Act a waterway is considered navigable if it is used as a highway for commerce for which trade and travel are or may be conducted in the customary modes of trade and travel on water. The waterway must form either by itself or united with other waterways to form a continued highway over which commerce is or may be carried out with other States or foreign countries in the customary modes in which such commerce is conducted by water. Prior to the 1880's there was no navigable water outlet from Lake Okeechobee to either the Atlantic or Gulf Coasts until Hamilton Disston dredged navigable connections to the Atlantic Ocean via the St. Lucie canal and to the Gulf of Mexico via the Caloosahatchee River. Therefore under the law, until the these connections were made, Fisheating Creek was not navigable because no water route linked it to other States or countries.

All parties agreed that Cowbone Marsh has blocked access up Fisheating Creek since about 1940 due to the growth of dense vegetation. However, Lykes contended that Cowbone Marsh has always blocked travel on Fisheating Creek even before 1940. The COE argued that a channel has always existed through Cowbone Marsh up until at least 1929 (the date of a previous COE survey on Fisheating Creek) but not after 1940. Thus to find the creek navigable it would have to be shown that it was navigable sometime between the late 1880's when the outlets to the Atlantic and Gulf were created and 1940 when the channel through Cowbone Marsh had become permanently blocked. Lykes contends Cowbone Marsh has never been navigable and the COE contends is was once navigable until about 1940.

One of the most interesting accounts provided during the trial was COE's claim of navigability based on a description of a canoe trip up Fisheating

Creek in 1842. This trip was taken by members of the U.S. Navy as part of a 60 day exploration of the Everglades region. The trip was headed up by Lieutenant John Rodgers who on April 12, 1842 filed an official report of the expedition. Regarding Fisheating Creek, Rodgers reported that: *"The Thlothlopopka or Fish-eating Creek, runs through an open prairie through which it serves as a drain. As might be expected, it gives evidence of being in the wet season a large stream, but when I examined it the volume of water it discharged was very small. This stream is very tortuous, and sometimes swells into a river, and then dwindles into a brook. Its head is in a marshy prairie, where a number of streamlets run together about twenty miles in a straight line, due east to the Okechobee, but following the course of the creek about twice that distance. The banks of the Fish-eating Creek are covered with game, and its waters filled with game."*

The expedition's details were recorded in a journal kept by one of the crew, George Preble. Preble's journal was published in 1883 in a report entitled, "A Canoe Expedition into the Everglades - 1842" based on his diary as well as the official report filed by Lieutenant Rodgers. Preble reported that the detachment consisted of 22 men in five 30 foot long dugout canoes made from hollowed out cypress logs which were paddled by the men and steered by a rudder. On February 13, 1842 the canoes entered the Everglades at Miami and proceed north to Ft. Lauderdale where they worked their way up New River west into the everglades. At night the men would sleep in their canoes.

On a cold day on February 22, they entered the southeast side of Lake Okeechobee where they sailed and paddled across the lake towards the northwest. On March 3 they entered Fisheating Creek where they camped a few miles up the mouth at Fort Center in Cowbone Marsh. During this expedition the men were also alert for the presence of Seminole Indians as the Second Seminole War was still underway and would not end for another five months.

Preble and the canoe expedition left Fort Center on March 5 and headed up Fisheating Creek where he reported they *"proceeded up the creek with great difficulty, pushing the canoes through the weeds, the creek for a space spreading out into a wide swamp"* (presumably after traveling through the head of Cowbone Marsh). On March 6 Preble reported *"After hauling the canoes over two troublesome places, re-entered the creek, a beautiful stream, with a clear, white sandy bottom. Pulled against the current to the Sd.* (south) *and the Wd* (west). *Saw immense flocks of cranes, pink spoonbills, curlew, and wild turkeys in plenty. Our camping-ground the prettiest by far that we have had. Two veteran cypress stretched their scraggy arms over our camp, draped in moss to the very ground. The day was rendered harmonious by the warbling of multitudes of feathered flocks of choristers, and the night hideous with the splash of alligators, hooting of owls, and screaming of a variety of unquiet night-birds."*

On March 7 Preble reported that they entered the headwaters of the creek where it *"loses itself in a swamp"*, so they headed back downstream as they shot at game along the way. That night Preble reported that they *"feasted sumptuously on wild turkey, broiled and fried curlew, plover and teal, stewed crane, Grecian ladies and fried fish, our spoils of the day"*. On March 8 they paddled all day until finally arriving back to Fort Center after dark. On March 10, they exited the creek into Lake Okeechobee and continued their journey up the Kissimmee River all the way to Lake Tohopekaliga near present day Kissimmee where they then made their way back, arriving in Miami on April 11.

Ironically, Preble's account resulted in two different conclusions. The COE and the State argued that the account supported their finding of navigability whereas Lykes and the district court found that the Preble account supported a finding of non-navigability. The COE also based their argument of navigability on historical maps and surveys which it said showed Cowbone Marsh was navigable. Lykes presented witnesses including two who were born as early as 1919 and who testified that they didn't ever remember Cowbone Marsh being navigable even as far back as the early 1920's. The 11th Circuit Court of Appeals ruled that the district court was correct in finding that Fisheating Creek was not navigable.

The State of Florida along with two local environmental groups, Save Our Creeks Inc. and The Environmental Confederation of Southwest Florida (represented by Earth Justice), then sued Lykes over the ownership issue in the State Court in Glades County and after months of deliberation a jury determined that Fisheating Creek in Glades County was sovereign land up to the ordinary high water line with title to be vested with the State. The Court's order awarded immediate possession of the creek to the State in spite of the fact that the ordinary high water line remarking the boundary between private land and sovereign land had not yet been determined.

Lykes then prepared to file an appeal, however, in order to prevent costly and time consuming litigation, the parties entered a Settlement Agreement. Rather than spend time and money trying to establish where the OHW line fell along the entire creek corridor within Glades County, the parties agreed per a Settlement Agreement for Lykes to quitclaim 8,387 acres along the creek proper to the State. The State would also purchase 9,781 acres adjacent to the quitclaim lands for a total of 18,168 acres. In addition, the Settlement Agreement resulted in the State purchase of a perpetual conservation easement over 41,606 acres of Lykes land referred to as Phase I Conservation Easement which allows Lykes to maintain their traditional agricultural uses of the land while ensuring that the current conditions and natural resource values are preserved.

FISHEATING CREEK WILDLIFE MANAGEMENT AREA

In 2003, per the 1999 Settlement Agreement, the Florida Department of Environmental Regulation (FDEP) approved the Conceptual Management Plan (CMP) for the Fisheating Creek Wildlife Management Area (WMA) encompassing 18,272 acres of State-owned land along the creek corridor from the Glades/Highlands County line to S.R. 78 near the mouth at Lake Okeechobee. FWC is the designated lead managing agency for the WMA and has procured a lease from the Trustees of the Internal Improvement Trust Fund to carry out its responsibilities. The lease calls for the FWC to "manage the leased premises only for the conservation and protection of natural and historical resources and resource-based, public outdoor recreation which is compatible with the conservation and protection of these public lands as set forth in subsection 253.023(11) Florida Statutes."

In addition, the Settlement Agreement contains other detailed management directives to the FWC in the WMA such as maintenance of a navigable channel within the creek, prohibition of jet ski's and jet boats, and restrictions on airboat use in the lower creek below Cowbone Marsh, including the ability to enact up to a one mile no airboat buffer around the swallowtail kite roost as needed. Prior to approval of the CMP the FWC held public hearings in Glades County to gain input from public and private interests on managing the WMA. This input was used by FWC to develop goals, objectives and strategies for the CMP. A final public hearing on the CMP was held in 2002. The WMA is now open to the public year round but access is restricted to persons on foot, bicycles and in boats. Designated entrances are located at the private concession run campground in Palmdale, at the end of Main Street in Palmdale, and at the public boat ramp off S.R. 78 near the mouth of the creek.

Limited hunting is also allowed during established hunting seasons on a portion of the WMA west of U.S. 27 during five separate short hunting seasons (35 days total) held between September 18 and April 5 during Archery, Black Powder and General Gun, General Gun Hog, and Spring Turkey seasons. In addition hunting is allowed east of U.S. 27 during two separate short hunting seasons (14 days total) held in March during Spring Gobbler season. Migratory Birds may be hunted west of U.S. 27 during WMA hunting seasons that coincide with the State Migratory Hunting seasons. Fishing and frogging are allowed year round both east and west of U.S. 27. Hunters must check in and out at the Palmdale Campground. During hunting periods, the FWC encourages non-hunters to camp at either the Palmdale Campground or at any of the four primitive creek front campgrounds located west of U.S. 27 or at one of the two primitive creek front campgrounds located east of U.S. 27.

In addition, approved canoe concessionaires are allowed to use Lykes property easements for canoe access at Ingram's Crossing via C.R. 731 and Burnt Bridge via S.R. 74, both access points located on the west side of the WMA. From Ingram's Crossing canoeist can paddle 16 miles to the Canoe Outpost and campground in Palmdale which normally takes two days with an overnight camp on the creek. From Burnt Bridge the trip is 8 miles and takes a full day to reach the campground. Canoeist can also go downstream from the campground east of U.S. 27 in Palmdale for approximately 9 miles providing the water levels are high, before the channel disappears. At this point the water sheet flows through a large open cypress slough before flowing into thick vegetation within Cowbone Marsh. The thick vegetation and lack of a channel in the Cowbone Marsh area has prevented Fisheating Creek from being completely navigable since at least 1940. Reportedly during high water the more adventurous canoeist and kayakers have traversed this area but it has been recommended that those attempting this first submit a travel plan with the Canoe Outpost, take a cell phone and GPS, and don't try it alone. Primitive camping is allowed anywhere on the 18,272 acres.

Many people may not be aware that this WMA has a long history and was originally opened to the public in the late 1940's through a cooperative agreement between Lykes and the FWC. When first opened, the WMA was massive and contained close to 125,000 acres of land west of Lake Okeechobee available for hunters, campers and other outdoor lovers. In 1966 the WMA boundary was amended to include a 100,000 acre wildlife refuge (where hunting was prohibited) located east of U.S. 27 and a 76,000 acre WMA located west of U.S. 27 where hunting was allowed. The WMA is known to have some of the best wild turkey habitat in the State if not the entire Country and bag limits were very liberal at that time with harvest of as many as 300 turkeys per season. For many years Lykes allowed the FWC to use the WMA as an experimental station or "living laboratory" to conduct extensive and valuable research on game species, especially the wild turkey within both the Fisheating Creek WMA and the Fisheating Creek Wildlife Refuge. This research was subsequently used for the management of this popular game species. Lykes also allowed the FWC to conduct research on the wild hog and the Florida sandhill crane.

Beginning about 1961, the FWC started experimenting with cannon nets to trap wild turkeys on Lykes property in order to restock the WMA as well as other areas of the State where turkeys had been eliminated from their original range. Up until this time, cannon nets had only been used in other states to trap waterfowl for banding and other research. Florida was one of a handful of States (Oklahoma, Texas, Missouri, West Virginia) that began experimenting with cannon nets in the 1960's to trap wild turkeys for restocking programs. Prior to cannon nets, turkeys in the WMA were trapped using pole traps, drop door traps or drugs, none of which were nearly as effective as cannon nets. After a few years of experimentation, use of the cannon net had been perfected and during the 1964-65 trapping season, four trained trappers with the FWC trapped an astounding 1,060 turkeys on Lykes property using a combination of cannon nets, drop door traps and drugs.

The procedure involved locating areas which were known to be used daily by turkeys. These areas needed to have large clearings nearby in order for the net to work. Blinds were built approximately 50 feet from the net where the trappers would be hidden. Dummy nets and traps were then placed at these sites so the turkeys would become accustomed to them. Bait (corn was preferred by turkeys) was then placed in the clearing just before daylight each morning. Once the turkeys began routinely feeding at the site it was time to trap, usually after about five days of continual use. Several sites were baited in order to choose the best site for trapping. The day before trapping was planned, the dummy nets and cannons were replaced with the working nets and cannons. Pre-made cartridges of black powder were used to power the three cannons which were placed on each end of the net as well as one in the center. The net consisted of a 50 X 60 foot nylon net with the trailing edge next to the cannons being staked down. The remainder of the net was fan folded so it would open up as the projectiles fired from the cannons pulled the leading edge over and across the flock of turkeys.

After some experimentation, it was determined that the optimal angle for the cannons was 17 degrees. The cannon charges were ignited with an electric charge provided by a 6 volt battery. The trappers arrived at the site well before daybreak and loaded the cannons. After firing the net, the trappers would run to the net and secure the turkeys by twisting a section of net over them so they would not injure themselves. The turkeys were then placed in boxes in the FWC vehicle where they would be banded and prepared for release at other sites. Some restocking sites were so remote that the FWC used slow flying fixed-wing aircraft to drop turkeys into them.

Another study of great importance conducted at the WMA concerned studying hunting harvest patterns of wild turkeys. The results of these studies convinced the FWC that the bag limits for turkeys were too high and needed to be more carefully controlled. Generally in Florida, turkey gobblers (males) are allowed to be hunted during the archery during the fall general gun hunting season on private lands and on a handful of public WMA's with a daily limit of one per day and two per season. During the spring gobbler season the bag limit is typically one per day and two per season. Up until the 1970's the bag limits for turkeys in Florida were drastically different than today, and on the Fisheating Creek WMA, during the general gun season, one turkey of either sex could be harvested per day with a season bag limit of 2, however a tagging system was not in place and it is likely that the season limit was not enforced very well.

Between 1949 and 1961, 331 turkeys were trapped and banded within the refuge area and released into the WMA area to study hunting harvest patterns. In the late 1960's the FWC suspected that bag limits were too liberal and that turkeys were being over harvested. Consequently, radio-tracking studies were conducted during six fall hunting seasons between 1967 through 1975 when 125 turkeys were banded and radio tracked in the WMA during the hunting seasons. During this study period, there was an average of 1,500 to 2,000 hunter visits in the WMA during the first week of the general gun hunting season each year and 5,000 to 6,000 total visits each season. This was prior to the enactment of the current quota system for public WMA's and there was no limit on the number of hunters allowed into the WMA during the first two weeks as there is today. The results of the study were dramatic. During the first few days of the season up to half the seasonal harvest had occurred and by the end of the first week up to 80% of the total harvest for the season had occurred.

The termination of the study resulted in several conclusions. During the 1971 through 1973 general gun seasons only gobblers were legal (no hens) and harvest rates drop significantly due to the fact that hunters had to determine the sex of the turkey before shooting. This helped to spread the harvest out throughout the season and allowed more hunters opportunities to kill a turkey other than just during the first week. However, during these three years, the number of illegally shot hen turkeys increased and by the 1973 season, five out of six hens radio monitored had been illegally killed. The FWC concluded that allowing fall hunting of gobblers was questionable in that the hunters did not seem capable of following the regulations.

The FWC also concluded that legal hunting could virtually eliminate the turkey population and that reducing the harvest of hen turkeys was required. In addition, effective turkey hunting regulations appeared to have a greater effect on turkey management over all other management practices including food plots and restocking. Following the radio tracking study on harvest patterns the FWC initiated new regulation in the WMA including allowing turkey hunting only a few days per week and with no more than 50 turkey hunters per day. The FWC reported that the turkey population on the WMA increased steadily thereafter without restocking or additional management practices.

THE FISHEATING CREEK ECOSYSTEM

Three weeks prior to the Settlement Agreement which determined that the State of Florida owned the Fisheating Creek corridor within Glades County, the Fisheating Creek Ecosystem in Glades and Highlands Counties was officially added to the Florida Forever land acquisition project list as a "less than fee" project through sponsorship by The Nature Conservancy. The total initial project size was 168,360 acres, all owned by Lykes and all located within Glades County with the exception of a 600 acre Lykes parcel located within Highlands County. In 2000, the 8,400 acre Smoak Groves parcel in Highlands County, also known as Venus Ranch, was added to the project boundary as an "less than fee" addition and the conservation easement was subsequently purchased. Two other smaller parcels within Glades County referred to as the Whidden parcel (.46 acres) and the Journigan Place parcel (115.4 acres), were added to the project boundary in 2002 and 2004 as fee simple additions.

Today with a few modifications, the total project size consists of around 176,875 acres of which about 68,174 acres have been purchased or protected with conservation easements. The Settlement Agreement resulted in fee simple ownership by the State of 18,168 acres along both sides of the entire creek corridor within Glades County referred to as the "Expanded Corridor". It includes 8,387 acres along the creek corridor below the Ordinary High Water (OHW) line determined to be owned by the State as well as an additional 9,781 acres above and adjacent to the OHW line which were purchased from Lykes per the Settlement Agreement. The Expanded Corridor runs from the Glades/Highlands County line on the north to the floodplain marsh (including Cowbone Marsh) located between the Herbert Hoover Dikes on the north and south sides of the creek west of S.R. 78.

In addition, the Settlement Agreement resulted in the purchase by the State of a perpetual conservation easement on 41,606 acres of Lykes land which is referred to as the Phase I Conservation Easement. The Phase I Conservation Easement allows Lykes to continue to own the land and maintain their traditional agricultural uses of the land while also ensuring through the easement that the current conditions and natural resource values are preserved. Finally, as mentioned, a conservation easement was purchased over the 8,400 acres of the Smoak Groves parcel located within Highlands County.

The Settlement Agreement also gave Lykes the option to sell to the State four additional conservation easements referred to as Phases II through V with a total acreage of 91,305 acres as well as a future potential conservation easement on 17,280 acres bounded on the north by C.R. 74 and on the west by the Glades/Charlotte County line.

Therefore the 176,875 acres encompassing the Fisheating Creek Ecosystem project includes: 18,168 acres of State owned fee simple ownership lands within the Expanded Corridor; 41,606 acres of Phase I conservation easement lands from the Lykes; 8,400 acres of conservation easements on the Smoak Groves parcel; 91,305 acres of potential Lykes conservation easements within Phases II through V; 17,280 acres of potential Lykes conservation easements on land located south of C.R. 74: and 116 acres of potential State fee simple lands known as the Whidden and Jourigan parcels. Of the total acreage in the project, 68,174 acres have been protected through either State fee simple acquisition or State acquisition of conservation easements and the remaining lands sought for conservation consists of 108,700 acres, all but 116 acres to be conservation easements.

The project summary for the Fisheating Creek Ecosystem states that the purpose of the acquisition is to preserve the land in order to link the Okaloacoochee Slough, Big Cypress Swamp, Babcock-Webb WMA, and Lake Okeechobee to ensure the survival of the Florida panther, swallowtail kite, other plants and animals that require such habitats, and to help complete the Florida National Scenic Trail. It is hoped that if lands within this project can be protected, they will eventually be part of one large contiguous conservation area running west to link up with the Babcock Ranch recently purchased by the State and to the FWC-owned Cecil Webb Wildlife Management Area, both in Charlotte County. The State would also like to ultimately connect these lands south into Hendry County to join up with the Okaloacoochee Slough State Forest and the Big Cypress National Preserve.

The summary goes on to say that the project area is important for the protection of rare plants and animals and is a Strategic Habitat Conservation Area for the panther, Florida grasshopper sparrow, swallow-tailed kite, Audubon's crested caracara, Everglades snail kite, mottled duck, Florida sandhill crane, red-cockaded woodpecker, short-tailed hawk, and the Southern bald eagle which has at least six nests within the project boundary. The Florida Natural Areas Inventory has identified 27 rare species of plants and animals associated with the project boundary. The summary finds also that the project contains 31 known archaeological sites, but that there may be more.

As mentioned above, in 2003 the State Trustees of the Internal Improvement Trust Fund (TIITF) approved purchase of a perpetual conservation easement on all 8,400 acres of the Smoak Groves Ranch. The Smoak Groves Ranch deserves special mention because of the Smoak family's generous efforts in helping to preserve the region's unique natural resources. The ranch is bounded on the west by U.S. 27 and on the south and east by the Glades County line and on the north by the Hendrie Ranch. Smoak Groves is primarily used for cattle ranching but there are also some limited sod and timber operations. The west side of the ranch includes the east slope of the Lake Wales Ridge and contains some of the last stands of bay swamp or baygall wetlands in the region which are favored by black bear for cover and denning. Land cover on the ranch consists of approximately 3,400 acres of improved pasture with the remaining 5,000 acres consisting of native habitats including scrub, cutthroat seeps, pine flatwoods, marsh and forested wetlands which includes the baygall wetlands. The Smoak's also own agricultural lands in Hardee and Marion County.

Pursuant to the easement agreement the ranch can continue to be used for hunting, fishing and to raise cattle. Timber harvesting may only occur in the future if improved pasture is converted to timber operations. No timber may be harvested in wetland areas and citrus is not an allowed use. An existing five acre borrow pit on the ranch can continue to be excavated for fill but no new mining or excavation can occur elsewhere on the ranch. The ranch also cannot be used for landfills or hazardous waste sites. In addition, the ranch may construct up to five additional residences with a minimum of 1,500 acres per residence.

Smoak Groves is also prime black bear habitat. Third generation rancher Mason Smoak developed a special friendship with bear researcher David Maehr, a wildlife biologist and professor with the University of Kentucky. Maehr was also a visiting scientist at the Archbold Biological Station (ABS), an ecological research facility located on about 8,600 acres of land containing scrub, pine flatwoods, cutthroat seeps, improved pastures and wetlands located just northwest of the Smoak Ranch west of US 27. ABS and the FWC have also been studying the Glades/Highlands sub-population of black bears for years. Maehr had previously spent years working for the FWC on the Panther Recovery Program as well as conducting research on black bears and other wildlife. He was passionate about protecting Florida's two large carnivores, the panther and the black bear. He also wrote over 120 wildlife articles and authored or co-authored several books, including *The Florida panther - Life and Death of a Vanishing Carnivore* (1997).

The Smoak family allowed Maehr the use of the ranch to conduct research on the sub-population of 100-150 black bears known as the Glades/Highlands sub-population which inhabit a core area of approximately 50,000 acres or 78 square miles in northern Glades County and southern Highlands County. The Smoak family provided use of their swamp buggies and ATV's and assisted David in capturing and collaring numerous bears on the ranch. Mason also flew Maehr in his small airplane so they could track the movements of bears they had collared with radio and satellite receivers.

In 2005, with Maehr's recommendation, Mason Smoak was presented with Disney's "Conservation Hero Award for North America" for his efforts to manage and protect the ecological integrity of the family's ranches and for his tremendous support of the black bear research project and increasing awareness of black bears in Highlands County. Tragically, in 2008, Smoak and Maehr were killed in a plane crash while completing aerial surveys of the Highlands County bear population. However, their work lives on forever and the University of Kentucky and ABS are continuing research on the Glades/Highlands sub-population of black bears.

As to the Phase I conservation easement over the Lykes land, it states *"the landowner (Lykes) and the easement owner (State) mutually recognize the natural, scenic and special characteristics of the Protected Property and have the common purpose of conserving certain natural values and character of the Protected Property by conveyance and acceptance of a Perpetual Conservation Easement on, over, and across the Protected Property, which shall preserve the value, character, ecological integrity, hydrological integrity of the Protected Property, conserve and protect the animal and plant populations, on the Protected Property, and prohibit certain further development activity on the Protected Property subject to provisions set forth herein."*

Five separate areas (A through E) within Phase I containing 35,000 acres were identified as "Natural Easement Areas" defined as *"areas containing habitats and natural communities that exhibit significant biological diversity, intact community structure and important species composition and have maintained their ecological integrity. These areas do not show substantial human-induced disturbance, including pollution and the establishment of invasive exotic plants and animals that cause damage to the ecological systems and landscape balance. These areas may require different management strategies."*

The Natural Easement Areas were briefly described as follows: Area A referred to as "Squirrel Tail" which contains 4,885 acres north and east of Fisheating Creek (west of U.S. 27) consisting of a mixture of dry and wet prairie, seepage slopes, mesic and wet flatwoods, scrub/scrubby flatwoods, bottomland/hardwood forests and longleaf pine important to red-cockaded woodpeckers, Florida sandhill crane, Florida scrub jay, short-tailed hawk, wading birds, Florida grasshopper sparrow, swallow-tailed kite, Audubon's crested caracara, Sherman's fox squirrel, Florida panther, and Edison's ascyrum and cutthroat grass.

Area B referred to as "Rainey Slough" which contains of 3,830 acres (east and west of C.R. 731) consisting of a vast floodplain marsh with open water channels, mesic hammock important to wading birds, including great egret, snowy egret, little blue heron, tricolor heron, white ibis, and wood stork.

Area C referred to as "Crane Island" which contains 10,329 acres (northwest of Lakeport) consisting of a large mosaic of wet and dry prairie, prairie hammocks, basin/depression marches important to Florida sandhill crane, short-tailed hawk, wading birds, Florida grasshopper sparrow, swallow-tailed kite, Audubon's crested caracara, eastern indigo snake, Florida panther, and Edison's ascyrum and cutthroat grass.

Area D referred to as "Hackletrap" which contains 12,046 acres (mostly north of Cowbone Marsh) characterized by mesic/wet flatwoods, prairie hammocks, floodplain marsh, dry and wet prairie, basin/depression marshes important to Southern bald eagle, Florida panther, Florida sandhill crane, short-tailed hawk, wading birds, Florida grasshopper sparrow, swallow-tailed kite, Audubon's crested caracara, eastern indigo snake and Edison's ascyrum and cutthroat grass.

Area E referred to as "Six Mile Marsh" which contains 3,822 acres (northwest of Lakeport) north of the Herbert Hoover Dike consisting of a huge basin marsh important to wading birds, swallow-tailed kite, and Florida sand hill crane.

The conservation easement agreement also identified seven areas of 6,500 acres referred to as "Impacted Easement Areas" described only as areas exhibiting substantial human-induced disturbance. These areas are scattered throughout the 41,606 acres and range in size from only 36 acres up to 2,485 acres with three located west of U.S. 27 and four east of U.S. 27.

The conservation easement agreement allows certain rights to be reserved by Lykes including the right to sell, lease or convey the property. However, the entire 41,606 acres of property may not be divided into more than twenty parcels containing one farmstead each and of the twenty parcels, a maximum of seven parcels may be divided within the 35,000 acres of Natural Easement Areas where each must be at least 2,500 acres in size. In addition, any farmsteads created may be no larger than 20 acres. Within the Impacted Easement Areas parcels must be at least 200 acres in size. Within both the Natural Easement Areas and Impacted Easement Areas, all buildings must be at least 500 feet from the nearest boundary of the 18,168.2 acre Expanded Corridor.

Other rights reserved by the Lykes include the right to continue "existing" agricultural uses and activities including cattle operations, haying and sodding (in Impacted Easement Areas 1 through 7 only), seed and fruit harvesting, and silviculture (no new silviculture activities will be allowed with the Natural Easement Areas). Lykes may also continue to allow hunting and fishing as well as the right to conduct ecotourism, subject to a State approved eco-tourism plan. Lykes may also explore and extract oil and gas from the property provided activities are conducted offsite, unless otherwise agreed by all parties that the activities are not intrusive and are temporary.

The conservation easement agreement prohibits the following activities: citrus activities; limits to pesticides and herbicides; deliberate introduction of exotic plants and animals; feedlots; haying and sodding in the Natural Easement Areas; truck/row crops; harvesting within wetlands including bald cypress, pond cypress, loblolly bay, red bay, black gum, red maple and other similar wetland tree species; mining, development of commercial well fields, alteration of natural water courses, and new construction (except that related to the farmsteads).

The Settlement Agreement also gives Lykes the option to sell to the State four additional conservation easements referred to as Phases II through V. Phase II consists of 27,823 acres located immediately west of Brighton Seminole Indian Reservation in the northeast portion of the project boundary; Phase III consists of 24,449 acres encompassing most of the Nicodemus Slough Drainage area located north of U.S. 27, south of Herbert Hoover Dike, and west of S.R. 78; Phase IV consists of 20,719 acres located between S.R. 74 on the south and the Glades Highlands County line to the north, the Glades/Charlotte County line on the west and C.R. 731 on the east; Phase V consists of 18,312 acres located in four separate parcels, two on the north and south sides of Rainey Slough and two others north of Fisheating Creek east and west of U.S. 27.

The Settlement Agreement contains a Management Plan for the Phase I conservation easement agreement. Lykes is allowed to stock cattle on the Protected Property at a rate of one animal per ten acres or a maximum of 4,161 head per year on the entire 41,606 acres. Lykes must adhere to the

United State Department of Agriculture's 1999 Cow/Calf Best Management Practices Guidelines, and Range Management for Important Native Grasses of Florida. Existing improved pastures can be maintained with chopping, mowing, burning, disking, fertilization, and re-seeding using the above Best Management Practices. Existing unimproved pastures may be improved only within IEA's. Endangered species must be managed according to FWC Guidelines. Existing eucalyptus plantations can be maintained but not expanded.

Harvesting of wild landscape plants including but not limited to wax myrtle, oaks, sabal palm, slash pine is permitted only in IEA's. Harvesting of wild landscape plants in NEA's will be allowed on a periodic basis by mutual agreement between the landowner and the easement monitor. Up to five existing permanent hunt camps located within the Expanded Corridor may be re-located to NEA B north of IEA 2 as well as IEA's 2 through 7. Up to twenty temporary hunt camps (tents and RV's) can be placed within the Protected Area with no more than seven located within the NEA's.

None of the headwaters area of Fisheating Creek within Highlands County has been included in the project boundary. The headwaters of Fisheating Creek are located at the western foot of the Lake Wales Ridge where groundwater and surface water from the ridge flow west into the headwaters. Numerous tributaries flow west from the ridge and ultimately form the main channel of Fisheating Creek which then flows south through Highlands County. This upper section of Fisheating Creek within Highlands County has received much less attention than the more heavily forested lower segment of the creek which flows through Glades County and which is now in public ownership. However, the Highlands County section of Fisheating Creek accounts for over half the length of the creek and also contains important wildlife habitats as well.

Much of Fisheating Creek within Highlands County has been channelized for flood control purposes and to facilitate agriculture, primarily cattle ranching and the dominate land cover is improved pasture. Ranches along this section of the creek have preserved much of the native habitats which support numerous rare and endangered plant and animal species including dry prairie, beautiful live oak hammocks, xeric scrub, and wetlands associated with Fisheating Creek. A FWC report identifies Strategic Habitat Conservation Areas (SHCA) for listed species of wildlife in the headwaters area including the Florida grasshopper sparrow, Audubon's crested caracara, Florida sandhill crane, Swallowtail kite, and the Florida burrowing owl. In addition the report identifies the Blue Head Ranch from S.R. 70 south as an area of containing "Important Prairie Lands" based on areas containing dry prairie, oak scrub and freshwater marsh along with habitats know to support prairie bird species.

A handful of private ranches occupy most of the land in the upper section of Fisheating Creek including: Blue Head Ranch, the largest with over 65,000 acres; Westby Ranch with approximately 10,237 acres; the Carlton Ranch with approximately 8,568 acres and the Waldron Ranch with approximately 2,425 acres. S.R. 70 is the only major road which traverses the upper creek from east to west and this section of the creek, even though channelized, still has a remote Old Florida feeling to it as does the more heavily forested southern section in Glades County.

Another small but important tract of public conservation land (not included within the Fisheating Creek Ecosystem project boundary) is in Highlands County just north of the Glades County line and is known as the Platt Branch Wildlife and Environmental Area (WEA). This parcel was originally known as the Johnson Ranch and in 1995 the FDOT purchased the entire 1,710 acre ranch as a wetland and upland conservation land bank or mitigation bank for State road projects and today the site contains 1,972 acres. Developers who impact Gopher Tortoise habitats on sites must pay into the State Mitigation Park Program and these funds are used to purchase sites such as the WEA.

The parcel had been suggested by The Nature Conservancy as an ideal site for a mitigation bank due to its diverse habitats which support 17 State and Federally protected animals species including the gopher tortoise, scrub jay, Sherman's fox squirrel, wood stork and the red-cockaded woodpecker. Florida panther and black bears are also known to occasionally visit the site. In addition, the site contains several rare and threatened plant communities including xeric oak scrub, cutthroat seeps and old growth longleaf pine flatwoods. This is the southern end of the longleaf pine habitat and this community is especially uncommon in this area. Cutthroat seeps are found in association with the side slopes of Central Florida's ridges and are named for the endemic Cutthroat Grass which grows on these moist areas.

The western portion of the WEA contains floodplain swamp associated with Fisheating Creek and the WEA is contiguous to the north side of the Fisheating Creek Ecosystem project boundary. The FWC now manages the site and is seeking to restore and improve habitats, with emphasis on the Gopher Tortoise, Florida scrub jay and red-cockaded woodpecker. The WEA is open to the public and access is provided via Detjens Road off U.S. 27. A hiking trail traverses through many of the habitats on the site and hikers may catch a glimpse of the red-cockaded woodpeckers.

The remainder of the creek channel in Glades County is unaltered and relatively pristine where it runs south and east through bottomland forest and floodplain swamp before passing through Cowbone Marsh then through a floodplain marsh west of SR 78 and ultimately discharging into Lake Okeechobee. The creek's drainage basin covers 918 square miles of land area. Of all the inflows to Lake Okeechobee including canals, rivers and creeks, Fisheating Creek is the only one whose water flow is not controlled by a water control structure. When the Herbert Hoover Dike around Lake Okeechobee was completed in the 1960's, it encircled the entire lake with the exception of Fisheating Creek where fortunately the two large dikes fan out on the north and south sides of the creek's floodplain west from Lake Okeechobee and adjacent to the large floodplain marsh where Ft. Center is located. This break in the dike precluded the need for a water control structure at the creek's mouth such as those found at the mouths of the Kissimmee River and Taylor Creek.

The majority of the Fisheating Creek Ecosystem has been owned by Lykes since the early 1900's where it has been managed primarily for cattle. As a result, land uses have remained low intensity and have been compatible with the habitat needs of many rare and endangered species as well as large populations of game species including white-tailed deer, wild hog, wild turkey, and bobwhite quail.

A 1994 FWC report entitled "Closing The Gaps In Florida's Wildlife Habitat Conservation System" (GAPS Report) identified the habitat areas in Florida that should be conserved in order to maintain key components of the State's biological diversity. The title refers to "gaps" identified in the statewide system of conservation areas that must be "closed" in order to maintain rare species of plants and animals as part of Florida's landscape. The report identifies "Strategic Habitat Conservation Areas" (SHCA), which are lands essential to providing some of the state's rarest animals, plants, and natural communities with the land base necessary to sustain populations into the future. The report also identified "Regional Biodiversity Hot Spots" (RBHS) or species rich areas where many rare or declining animals, plants, and natural communities were known to be assembled and was based on a large database of animals, plants, and natural communities. The purpose of including the RBHS maps in the GAPS Report was to identify habitat areas essential to the continued survival of rare and declining species not adequately protected by existing conservation areas. SHCA areas and RBHS cover most of the Fisheating Creek Ecosystem.

A 2009 addendum to the GAPS report entitled "Wildlife Habitat Conservation Needs in Florida - Updated Recommendations for Strategic

Habitat Conservation Areas" states that the Southwest Florida region (which includes Glades County) probably represents the most important region in Florida in terms of maintaining several wide-ranging species (i.e. - Florida panther, black bear, swallowtail kite, Florida sandhill crane, Audubon's crested caracara, etc.) that make up an important component of wildlife diversity in Florida. The report goes on to say that the region has the only stable population of Panthers east of the Mississippi River; the only stable population of black bear south of Lakeland Florida; the greatest concentration of Audubon's crested caracara in all of the U.S.; and supports core populations of Florida sandhill cranes, swallowtail kites and Florida burrowing owls.

The region to either side of Fisheating Creek represents a large area of land cover that is potentially important to many rare species. Many rare species have been documented in the SHCA associated with the Fisheating Creek Ecosystem within the mix of wet and dry prairies, cypress swamps, pinelands, unimproved pastures, upland hardwood forests, as well as the marshes and unimproved pastures of the lower creek west of SR 78.

The list is extensive and includes Florida panther, Sherman's fox squirrel, gopher tortoise, eastern indigo snake, south Florida rainbow snake, Edison's ascyrum, red-cockaded woodpecker, Florida sandhill crane, short-tailed hawk, Florida grasshopper sparrow, American swallowtail kite, Audubon's crested caracara, Florida scrub jay, Southern bald eagle, white ibis, wood stork, tri-colored heron, Florida burrowing owl, limpkin, mottled duck, little blue heron, and great egret. Other listed species within the Fisheating Creek Ecosystem are the gopher frog, the snowy egret, Artic peregrine falcon, Southeastern American kestral, Everglades snail kite, and Florida black bear. Five bald eagle nests have been recorded north of Cowbone Marsh and one south of Rainey Slough and two wading bird rookeries are located north of Cowbone Marsh.

The bulk of the Fisheating Creek Ecosystem project lands are located between the Glades/Highlands County line on the north and an east west line formed by S.R. 74 and U.S. 27 on the south. One part of the ecosystem boundary containing approximately 17,280 acres is found south of S.R. 74 in western Glades County adjacent to the Charlotte County boundary. Curiously, no other lands were recommended for inclusion in the Fisheating Creek Ecosystem project south of S.R. 74 and U.S. 27 even though these areas contain vast expanses of dry prairie and are known habitat for many listed species of animals. According to the FWC GAPS Report, an area referred to as "Ortona/Citrus Center/Hall City" bounded on the south by C.R. 78, on the west by C.R. 731 and on the north and east by S.R. 74 and

U.S. 27 is a SHCA for a large number of animal species including Florida panther, Florida black bear, Sherman's fox squirrel, Audubon's crested caracara, Florida scrub jay, wood stork, swallowtail kite, Southern bald eagle, Florida burrowing owl, mottled duck, eastern indigo snake and gopher tortoise. This area contains approximately 56,000 acres and all of it is owned by Lykes with the exception of approximately 6,500 acres north of Citrus Center.

Another area referred to by the GAPS Report as "Jack's Branch and Bee Branch" bounded on the north by S.R. 74, on the east by C.R. 731 on the south by C.R. 720 and on the west by the Glades County line, also contains SHCA for Florida panther, Sherman's fox squirrel, Audubon's crested caracara, Florida scrub jay, wood stork, Swallowtail kite, Southern bald eagle, Florida burrowing owl, Florida grasshopper sparrow, limpkin, Florida sandhill crane, great egret, Florida mottled duck, eastern indigo snake and gopher tortoise. This area is all owned by Lykes and contains approximately 36,000 acres. These two areas should be considered for addition to the project boundary for Fisheating Creek Ecosystem. In addition, these areas have been included in the FEGN Big Cypress/Fisheating Creek Critical Linkage which connects Fisheating Creek to Big Cypress Swamp and includes the Caloosahatchee Ecoscape Florida Forever Project where panthers have been know to cross the river dispersing into Glades County.

Another important feature of the Fisheating Creek Ecosystem is Nicodemus Slough, a tributary to Lake Okeechobee and part of the Fisheating Creek Ecosystem Florida Forever project known as Phase III potential conservation easement. Nicodemus Slough is located south of the Herbert Hoover Dike and north of the Lykes dike or more formally, Levee 306 and it flows east for approximately seven miles until it crosses under S.R. 78 via two separate drainage structures, discharging into Lake Okeechobee. The current drainage area of the slough encompasses approximately 25,000 acres and is bounded on the north, east, and west by the Herbert Hoover Dike and on the South by the Seaboard Coastline Railroad tracks. No doubt the original drainage area was larger prior to construction of the Herbert Hoover Dike and the Seaboard Railroad. The lower or eastern portion of the drainage area contains wetlands and the upper or western portion consists of improved pasture, dry prairie, and oak and palm hammocks.

The upland portions of the drainage basin on its west side, particularly the dry prairie habitats have been identified by FWC as Strategic Habitat for the American swallowtail kite, Audubon's crested caracara, Florida sandhill crane, Florida panther, Florida black bear and as important prairie lands based on known habitats for numerous prairie bird species. The wetland areas are know to be used as a foraging area by kites using the large swallowtail kite summer roost located adjacent to Nicodemus Slough just north of the Herbert Hoover Dike on the Fisheating Creek WMA. In addition, six archaeological sites have been documented within the drainage basin including one referred to as the Nicodemus Earthwork Site which is one of the largest know pre-historic Indian mound and earthwork complexes in South Florida. This site is located south of the L-306 levee and is now surrounded by intensive agricultural uses, primarily sugarcane.

The lower or eastern portion of the slough has always flooded periodically whenever Lake Okeechobee water levels are high and water backs up into the slough through the culverts under S.R. 78. The lake stages were increased in the late 1980's to 17.5 feet, aggravating the problem further and flooding crops and pasture lands within the southern and western portions of the drainage area. The flooding impacted agricultural uses in the drainage district. The Central and Southern Florida Flood Control District (the predecessor to SFWMD) and the U.S. Army Corps. of Engineers first considered flood control improvements for Nicodemus Slough back in 1959 when it was added to the Central and Southern Florida Flood Control District's project list.

The western portion of the drainage area consists of improved pasture, dry prairie, and oak and palm hammocks. Alternate structural plans were discussed to address the flooding problem with varying costs and environmental impacts. In 1986 SFWMD published the "Nicodemus Slough/C19 Project Conceptual Design Report. The report identified structural improvements needed to prevent high water and flooding in the slough as a result of high water in Lake Okeechobee.

These improvements have been constructed and include an east/west canal/levee system (L-306) across the lower drainage area between S.R. 78 on the east and the Seaboard Coastline Railroad on the west. Drainage canals and water control structures have also been constructed on the east and south portions of the drainage area to facilitate drainage into Lake Okeechobee and Lake Hicpochee during high water levels. South of the L-306 dike, the slough has been converted to intensive agriculture land.

Nicodemus Slough has also be targeted by the SFWMD as one of the alternative sites for a large 17,000 acre plus Stormwater Treatment Area where water runoff from the Fisheating Creek drainage basin would be stored to both control lake levels in Lake Okeechobee and to provide a treatment area for the excess nutrients (primarily phosphorus) which the basin has historically discharged into Lake Okeechobee. This will be discussed in the Water Quality chapter.

THE FLORIDA ECOLOGICAL GREENWAYS NETWORK

Before discussing the Fisheating Creek Ecosystem in more detail, it is important to first understand the significance of its geography. The Fisheating Creek Ecosystem is important not only because of its habitats and wildlife species but also because of its strategic location which is critical to the success of another conservation effort, a statewide ecological greenway network. Even before passage of the 1985 Growth Management Act, Florida's environmental community and government leaders were discussing another form of de-facto growth management, namely a Statewide greenway system. In 1991 these discussions came to some fruition when then Governor Lawton Chiles appointed the Florida Greenways Commission (FGC) to investigate the feasibility of a Statewide greenways system that included an ecological as well as a recreation component.

In 1994 the FGC recommended adoption of a statewide program that protected a system of trails and a functionally connected network of conservation lands to protect Florida's natural and rural landscapes. This program was to be administered by the Florida Department of Environmental Protection (FDEP), Office of Greenways and Trails. In 1995 the University of Florida was contracted to develop a Geographic Information System (GIS) system to help identify the best opportunities for both an ecological network and a recreational network.

The ecological network was to be referred to as the Florida Ecological Greenways Network (FEGN). This was a collaborative process overseen by three separate State appointed Greenway Councils and technical input was obtained from various stakeholders in over 20 sessions including the Florida Greenways Commission, the Florida Greenways Coordinating Council, state, regional and Federal agencies, scientists, university personnel, conservation groups, planners, and the general public. The FEGN model was then reviewed thoroughly in public hearings held throughout the State. The original FEGN was completed on July of 1998 using numerous GIS layers of data to identify large connected areas of ecologically significant habitat Statewide.

The results indicated that approximately 50% of the State was potentially suitable for inclusion within a statewide greenways system. With such a large area to consider, the University of Florida was asked to prioritize areas within the FEGN based on the relative significance of features within the network. This was done with a two step process. First, stakeholders were asked to identify criteria to use in prioritizing these areas into high, moderate and low priority. Second, stakeholders were asked to add another set of more detailed criteria for ranking areas identified as high and moderate priority. These refined criteria were needed to both support implementation of the Florida Greenways Program and as a way to prioritize potential conservation areas for inclusion in the Florida Forever Program.

The refined criteria included four priority classes: 1. Potential importance for maintaining or restoring wide-ranging species (e.g., Florida panther and black bear); 2. Importance for maintaining a statewide, connected reserve network from South Florida through the Florida panhandle; 3. Other important landscape linkages in support of higher priority linkages; and 4. Importance as a riparian corridor. The application of this criteria resulted in six priority classes. The FEGN also identified critical linkages, those more defined areas necessary to protecting the FEGN and prioritized based on ecological importance and threat from conversion to development.

The FEGN has been updated once and re-prioritized twice since its original version, based on updated land use information such as deletion of areas that have been developed or adding additional lands that meet the criteria for large connected areas of ecological significance, or adding lands containing habitat which could or does support threatened or endangered species. Data used to make changes to the FEGN was obtained from many cooperating public agencies and private conservation organizations. The FEGN is also being used as a core data layer in the Critical Lands and Waters Identification Project, which is a collection of statewide ecological GIS data used as a decision support tool for state, regional, and local conservation and land use planning. Starting in July 2010, the FEGN was subjected to a comprehensive update with a re-analysis of state core conservation areas and best opportunities to protect functional connectivity statewide.

This brings us to the Fisheating Creek Ecosystem. Twenty-four original areas were selected within the State as critical linkages or segments to the FEGN. Two of these centered on the Fisheating Creek Ecosystem and were referred to as the Big Cypress-Fisheating Creek Critical Linkage and the Fisheating Creek-Highlands Hammock Critical Linkage. From the original twenty four areas, the University of Florida in conjunction with The Nature Conservancy, selected ten which were subsequently approved in 2002 by the Florida Greenways and Trails Council. Number ten on the list was the Big Cypress-Fisheating Creek Critical Linkage which has been given a top priority ranking of 1 on a scale of 1 (highest) to 7 (lowest) and significantly, it is considered one of the three most important linkages in the State of Florida.

The Big Cypress-Fisheating Creek Critical Linkage is comprised of 775,000 acres.   It connects Big Cypress Swamp National Preserve, Everglades National Park and Corkscrew Swamp Sanctuary to the Fisheating Creek Ecosystem, The South Florida Water Management Districts Bright Hour Watershed conservation area (conservation easement), the Babcock Ranch State Preserve, and the FWC-owned Cecil Webb Wildlife Management Area.   It incorporates most of the FWC designated Strategic Habitat Conservation Areas (SHCA) for the Florida panther including the land within the Caloosahatchee Ecoscape project boundary known to be used previously by several panthers to cross the Caloosahatchee River as they have dispersed north into Central Florida.   It is thought that this crossing is essential for helping to re-establish a breeding population of panthers north of the river and to serve as a link for black bears in Big Cypress Swamp Preserve to the bears in the Glades/Highlands sub-population of black bears.

Additionally, the Florida Greenways Council reports that the Panther Glades, Twelve Mile Slough, Caloosahatchee Ecoscape, and Fisheating Creek Ecosystem Florida Forever Projects are essential to completing this linkage, and should be given high conservation priorities. The southwest portion of this linkage is threatened by moderate and high growth pressure from the expanding urban areas of Ft. Myers and LaBelle.   The Florida Greenways Council noted that highway underpasses may be needed along U.S. 27, and State Roads 29, 78, and 80, especially where these roads are proposed for widening within the Critical Linkage.

The Florida Greenways Council stated that even though the Fisheating Creek-Highlands Hammock Critical Linkage was important and was originally ranked as one of the 24 Priority Critical Linkages, the only reason it was not selected for the final list was that at that time it was considered to have lower development pressure than the linkages ultimately selected.   This decision was made in 2002, and since that time a major development, the Blue Head Ranch, a "New Town" (to be discussed later in this book), has been approved within the Fisheating Creek/Highlands Hammock Critical Linkage in southern Highlands County.

The Fisheating Creek/Highlands Hammock Critical Linkage connects the Fisheating Creek Ecosystem to an area within Highlands County as far north as Highlands Hammock State Park which is known to be the habitat for a sub-population of Florida black bear known as the Glades/Highlands sub-population. Biologist know that the genetic variability of this population is low due to their isolation and that their long term survival is dependent upon a connection to other populations, especially the Big Cypress population of black bear farther south.

In addition to these critical linkages, numerous regional corridors were identified by the FEGN as the most important in the State including The Big Cypress Preserve to Ocala National Forest Landscape Linkage which includes the Fisheating Creek Ecosystem. The Big Cypress to Ocala corridor is described as a critical regional landscape that will ensure a functional ecological network from south to north Florida containing vast ranch lands in Florida's Final Frontier which are compatible with biological diversity and ecological connectivity. These ranches are threatened by development spreading south of Orlando and inland from both coast. Focal species requiring large habitats that will benefit include the Florida panther, Florida black bear, Audubon's crested caracara, and Florida sandhill crane. This corridor as proposed would connect the Ocala National Forest in north Central Florida to the Big Cypress Swamp. The Big Cypress to Ocala corridor includes a key linkage of the Glades/Highlands sub-bear population to the Big Cypress bear population.

A recent spin off of the FEGN is known as the Florida Wildlife Corridor project which was officially established on Earth Day, April 22, 2010. The Florida Wildlife Corridor was founded by Dr. Tom Hoctor, Director of the Center for Landscape and Conservation Planning at the University of Florida and Carlton Ward Jr, Conservation Photographer and founder of the Legacy Institute for Nature & Culture (LINC). The idea was first proposed by Carlton Ward, an eighth generation Florida rancher in Central Florida, as a vision to connect, protect and restore natural ecosystems between Everglades National Park and Okefenokee Swamp in southeast Georgia. The goal of the Florida Wildlife Corridor project is a campaign to link the various corridor/ecological greenways project together into one grand landscape corridor project for peninsular Florida and to increase awareness of politicians, the public and policy makers of the importance to the future of Florida's people and wildlife. In addition, the campaign will stress that this initiative will not be achieved through increased land use regulation but through incentives to reward landowners who practice good stewardship on their ranches.

Florida now has a large informational database of locations of strategic habitats for wildlife, life histories and biological hotspots of endangered and threatened animal species, location of ecological greenways, and critical linkages within these greenways. Unfortunately, all of these studies and valuable data will have been a waste of time unless the lands identified in the studies can be preserved in perpetuity through one or more of the host of conservation initiatives available today while there is still time.

DRY PRAIRIE

Dry Prairie is endemic to central interior peninsular Florida and it comprises approximately 30% (43,000 acres) of the habitat within the Fisheating Creek Ecosystem boundary. Historically it occurred on several disjunct areas: (A). Along the Kissimmee River north of Lake Okeechobee in a physiographic region known as the Okeechobee Plain; (B) In an extensive area west of Lake Okeechobee known as the Desoto Plain and; (C) Portions of Sarasota and southern Manatee Counties. Other areas formally described as dry prairie such as along the upper reaches of the St. Johns River are now considered to be wet prairie associated with floodplain or seasonally flooded ponds and marshes. Dry prairie can describe a number of different vegetative communities.

According to the "Guide to the Natural Communities of Florida" published by the Florida Natural Areas Inventory (FNAI) dry prairie is defined as a nearly treeless plain found only in south/Central Florida consisting of a dense ground cover of wiregrass, saw palmetto, dwarf live oak, and other grasses, herbs and low shrubs. Many of the threatened and endangered plant and animal species found within the Final Frontier including the Fisheating Creek Ecosystem are there because of the extensive dry prairie habitat.

This community once covered over two million acres in Central Florida prior to settlement when it began to be converted into improved pasture for cattle grazing, agriculture, citrus and sod farms. Estimates of the amount of pre-settlement dry prairie are difficult to determine and vary widely. Some researchers believe that the amount of dry prairie existing in pre-settlement Florida was as much as two million acres. FNAI believes that there were approximately 1.2 million acres of pre-settlement dry prairie in Florida. J. W Harshberger appears to be the first to map the dry prairies in Florida in 1914 and he described the largest typic prairie as that which occurred in an area from north of the Caloosahatchee River, along the western shore of Lake Okeechobee, east of Peace Creek (River), bisected by Fisheating Creek and centered on Citrus Center (in southern Glades County). He described this area as "a prairie grass formation with sod-forming grasses, and some palmetto hammocks." Dry Prairie forms on nearly level, poorly to somewhat poorly drained inter-drainage flatlands above major river/stream floodplain valleys. The hardpan soils often found beneath dry prairie can result in short term flooding during the wet season or during winter storms with water sheet flowing for up to a month before draining off.

According to the FWS the most reliable method to determine the amount of pre-settlement dry prairie is through the original Public Land Surveys completed between 1855 and 1859. Although not quantified, most of these surveys show the boundary between prairie and pinelands on the original survey plats and since this was prior to any significant logging in Central Florida, the FWS believes these surveys are a fairly accurate depiction of the extent of the pre-settlement dry prairie habitats. Once settlement occurred and natural fire frequency had been reduced, areas of dry prairie not converted to other uses were probably invaded by pines.

Typical plants can include broomsedge, carpet grass, runner oak, Indian grass, love grass, blazing star, rabbit tobacco, pine lily, marsh pink, milkwort, goldenrod, musky mint, pawpaw, dwarf wax myrtle, gallberry, stagger bush, fetter bush, and dwarf blueberry. The lack of streams and creeks, which act as de-facto fire breaks in this community, appears to promote large scale periodic fires. The incidents of periodic fire as well as temporary flooding seems to keep the dry prairie relatively free from invasion by woody plants such a pines and oaks.

The FWS points out that the term "dry prairie" is a misnomer and typical dry prairie is a mixture of upland and wetland plants. The FWS describes dry prairie as: wiregrass, scattered areas of low stunted saw palmetto, and low growing runner oak interspersed with seasonally flooded ponds and marshes containing a variety of wetland plants including sawgrass, cord grass, pickerel weed, maiden cane, flag, water lily, etc. and mesic hammocks containing cabbage palm and/or oak trees, with very few surface water drainage features other than slough or swale drainage systems. However, there is significant local differences in composition and dominance of plant species in dry prairie depending on elevation, soil type and hydrology.

Dry Prairie has some of the highest species diversity of any habitat in Florida. A 1995 study sampled 17 plots and found an average of 22 plant species. The numerous plant species include all of the dry habitat species, all of the wetland species, as well as a diverse number of plant species found in the transitional areas between these two habitats. Due to the lack of streams in the dry prairie habitats, surface water not captured in depression marshes and ponds is drained by linear swales with short hydro-periods and by sloughs which tend to have deeper water and longer hydro periods. Prairie Hammocks consisting of cabbage palms and/or live oaks are a small component of the dry prairie but serve as important bio-diversity and are often found in proximity to wetlands. These hammocks often have ground cover damaged by cattle and/or wild hogs which use these sites for food and cover.

Many species of vertebrates inhabit the dry prairie year round or seasonally. Numerous migratory bird species use the dry prairie during the winter months including the Savannah sparrow, swamp sparrow, Henslow's sparrow, and the northeastern species of grasshopper sparrow, yellow rail and palm warbler. Winter birds of prey include the Northern harrier, Southeatern American kestral and various hawk species. The GAPS Report refers to "prairie birds" associated with the dry prairie habitats found in south and Central Florida. These include the Southern bald eagle, red-cockaded woodpecker, Florida sandhill crane, short-tailed hawk, Florida grasshopper sparrow, Florida scrub jay, American swallowtail kite, Audubon's crested caracara, mottled duck, limpkin, Everglades snail kite, and Florida burrowing owl. Because most of these birds are rare, the dry prairie, and it's associated depression marshes, wet prairies, and cabbage palm hammocks is one of the most important wildlife habitats remaining in Florida.

However, dry prairie has been in decline since the early 1900's due to conversion to agriculture (citrus, sugarcane, improved pasture) and urban development. Some researchers believe as much as 88% of the original dry prairie in Central Florida has been converted into other uses, historically for improved pasture for cattle but more recently for urban development and citrus. Others claim that about 19 percent of the original dry prairie remains, covering approximately 385,000 acres. On lands bordering Fisheating Creek within Glades County, some of the dry prairie has been roller chopped for pasture or converted into Eucalyptus plantations. Florida Dry Prairie is ranked by FNAI as Globally Imperiled and some researchers believe only 2 percent of the original ungrazed dry prairie remains.

Within the Final Frontier, there are five protected conservation areas with significant areas of dry prairie: Kissimmee Prairie State Preserve (23,000 acres, the largest); Myakka River State Park (17,000 acres); Three Lake Wildlife Management Area (10,000 acres); Avon Park Air Force Range (6,000, acres); and National Audubon's Kissimmee Prairie Sanctuary (2,500 acres). In addition, the Southwest Florida Water Management District has a conservation easement on 31,988 acres of the privately owned Bright Hour Ranch in Desoto County which protects 13,387 acres of dry prairie. Biologists estimate that 30 percent of the 176,876 acre Fisheating Creek Ecosystem project consists of dry prairie habitat, or 43,000 acres of dry prairie, significantly more than any of the above conservation areas.

There is an opportunity to restore disturbed dry prairie on public lands as well as on private lands where conservation easements can be obtained. Unimproved or semi-native pasture is the easiest to restore to native rangeland and since these communities have typically never been plowed, it is more likely that a native seed bank still exists within the soil column. The FWS has identified dry prairie as one of the 18 endangered ecological plant communities listed in the "Multi-Species Recovery Plan for South Florida" and has included recovery criteria. The FWS believes that the first priority to restoring dry prairie should be restoration of ecological functions including periodic fire and restoration of hydrology followed by managing rangeland and livestock grazing practices, control of exotic plants and animals and impacts of mechanical treatments.

Fire management is the most significant factor in determining vegetation structure and composition of the dry prairie habitats. Dry prairie without frequent fire often loses its natural ground cover to invading pines, oaks and shrubs, including saw palmetto. Frequent fire keeps saw palmetto stunted and sparsely distributed which is the normal condition for saw palmetto in dry prairies and studies have shown that Florida grasshopper sparrows prefer recently burned dry prairie over fire suppressed dry prairie

Hydrology strongly determines plant composition in the dry prairie. Historically it is believed that sheet flow was a common occurrence in the dry prairie during and after high rainfall events. Alteration of hydrology from ditching and diking can cause saw palmetto to convert to more wetland species from too much water, or in cases where water is drained, vegetation can change from wetland species to more woody upland species.

Between 1940 and 1960 many areas of native pasture and dry prairie were converted to Bahia, Bermuda and Bermuda grass. By 1985 it is estimated that 3.5 million acres of pine flatwoods and dry prairie had been converted into improved pasture and there were over 2 million head of cattle and calves. Florida still has some of the largest cow/calf ranches in the entire Country. However, Florida's native rangeland is not particularly high in nutritional value.

Florida's long growing season and high rainfall contribute to growing ample forage on improved pastures. Native rangeland is often burned by ranchers once or twice per year in the winter and/or early spring during times when forage is sparse and this burning produces new growth which is two to four times more nutritional than pre-burn growth. Burning also benefits native wildlife and controls invading shrubs. Studies seem to show that moderate grazing can increase plant species diversity but overgrazing can reduce plant species diversity and increase exotic species.

Dry Prairie can be mechanically treated through bedding, root raking, discing, roller chopping, plowing, etc. Bedding is often done prior to planting pines or eucalyptus. Rollerchopping is the most common mechanical treatment used on dry prairie to control shrubs, especially saw palmetto. Ironically, rollerchopping along with burning has also been found to be helpful in restoring dry prairie that has been mechanically altered.

Dry Prairie which has been converted to improved pasture such as Bahia or Bermuda grass can be encroached upon by other exotic grasses such as Tropical soda apple and carpet grass and these are often hard to eliminate once established. The most harmful of the exotic species is the wild feral hog which can root up many acres of dry prairie and improved pasture and these areas can then become more vulnerable to invasion by other exotic plants. However, feral hogs are here to stay and they will never be eliminated only controlled through trapping and hunting. Thus, wild hogs on private property are legal game year round in Florida.

WATER QUALITY IN FISHEATING CREEK

Fisheating Creek is often described as the only free flowing tributary to Lake Okeechobee because there are no water control structures to regulate water flows and water levels unlike the Kissimmee River and Taylor Creek on the lake's north side. However, this does not mean that the creek has not been altered because there have been extensive alterations in the upper section of the creek located primarily in southern Highlands County.

Up until recently, the creek's more open and marshy upper section, including the headwaters, have received much less attention than the lower section of the creek even though the upper section consists of over the half the length of the entire creek. The upper section runs approximately 20 miles, from just south of S.R. 66 on the north to the C.R. 731 bridge near Venus on the south. Most of this section has been channelized for flood control to accommodate agriculture and there is an extensive system of drainage ditches and canals with at least two water control structures, a check dam and a drop spillway.

According to the South Florida Water Management District (SFWMD), the USGS maps created in 1953 and updated in 1984 indicate that the far northern areas of the watershed, where the headwaters of the creek are located, include vast areas of marsh bisected by a system of ditches and canals. SFWMD states that "it is likely that a more extensive marsh system existed in the upstream headwaters of Fisheating Creek in 1953 than were present in 1984 or in the current time". And in a 2006 Water Quality Assessment Report for the Kissimmee River and Fisheating Creek, DEP states that "In its natural state, Fisheating Creek inundated large areas of marsh during the wet season. As agriculture moved into the area, some wetlands were drained and the main channel artificially widened."

Historical aerial photo's show that ditching activities were ongoing on the Blue Head Ranch property in the upper creek including channelization of Fisheating Creek and excavation of a large ditch through the large unnamed marsh located northeast of the ranch. The 1950's aerials show that ditching had continued including more connections under S.R. 70 and north within Fisheating Creek. In addition the 1950's aerials show new farm fields and pastures north of S.R. 70. In 1970 the aerials revealed additional farm fields and pastures both north and south of S.R. 70.

In 1954 Congress authorized the Watershed Protection and Flood Prevention Act of 1954 also known as the Small Watershed Program, to be administered by the Department of Agriculture, Soil Conservation Service

(SCS), predecessor to the National Resource Conservation Service.   The Small Watershed Program was created to provide technical and financial assistance (cost sharing) to local sponsors to develop and implement watershed plans for watershed protection, flood prevention, agricultural and non-agricultural water management, and groundwater recharge.   SCS projects are subsidized mostly with Federal funds   and   limited local funding.   The early years of the program focused on assistance in watershed protection, flood damage reduction and agricultural drainage primarily through building drainage channels.

In 1957, the Small Watershed Program authorized a project in the headwaters of Fisheating Creek known as "Fisheating Creek Marsh" which consisted of drainage improvements on 51,200 acres of land.   The project resulted in creation of a network of drainage ditches and canals as well as a check dam and a drop spillway on the creek.   This project undoubtedly resulted in the rapid increase in agricultural activities in the upper section of Fisheating Creek as noted by the SFWMD. The Fisheating Creek sub-watershed encompasses the entire drainage area of the creek   from the headwaters in Highlands County to the mouth of the creek at Lake Okeechobee and covers almost 440 square miles.   The Fisheating Creek sub-watershed has been identified as one of the most significant sources of phosphorous loading to Lake Okeechobee of all the nine sub-watersheds draining into the lake.   Phosphorous, which is a nutrient, has resulted in an increase in algae blooms in the lake and has contributed to eutrophication in the lake.

In addition, phosphorous laden water discharged from Lake Okeechobee to tide through the Caloosahatchee and St. Lucie Rivers has caused algae blooms in both rivers and their estuaries.   The water quality of Fisheating Creek has been adversely affected by agricultural activities in the upper reaches of the creek.   Studies by the SFWMD show that between 1984 and 2006 more than 72 square miles (46,080 acres) of rangeland (unimproved pasture with native vegetation) was converted to farmland in the Fisheating Creek Sub-basin for farming, citrus and cattle production.   Most of this work was done in Highlands County but some was also located in the downstream section within Glades County.

Prior to settlement of Florida, Lake Okeechobee had relatively low levels of phosphorous.   However, the major land use in the Okeechobee watershed is now agriculture with cattle ranching being the most common form of agriculture.   The top five cattle producing Counties in Florida are: Okeechobee, Highlands, Osceola, Polk, and Hendry.   Florida cattle ranches run cow/calf operations where calves are raised until they reach a weight of

400 to 500 pounds, then they are weaned from their mothers and shipped to feedlots primarily in Texas, Oklahoma, Kansas and Alabama. These states produce significantly more feed than Florida.

Phosphorous levels have tripled in Lake Okeechobee since the 1960's. The main source of phosphorous is runoff from cattle ranches and dairy farms. However, unlike dairy farms, beef cattle ranches are not considered a source of point source pollution due to their lower animal stocking rates and are therefore not subject to regulations from Federal and State agencies. Even though phosphorous runoff rates from cattle ranches are relatively low compared to more intensive agriculture, this is offset by the vast acreage of this land use. Studies have shown that much of the phosphorous entering Lake Okeechobee is what has been termed "legacy fertilizer" which is fertilizer that is slowly leaching out of the soil from previous annual applications of fertilizer onto Bahia grass, the dominate pasture grass planted on improved pastures (70%). This phosphorous has accumulated in the soil over the years and is now leaching into surface water. Studies indicate that even on pastures where fertilization was stopped over 15 years ago, phosphorus is still leaching into downstream water bodies.

Today, the University of Florida's Institute of Food and Agricultural Science (IFAS) now recommends against annual fertilization of Bahia and only recommends fertilization of Bahia during the first year of planting. Other grasses which account for the remaining 30% of pasture grasses still need annual fertilization however.

Land uses identified as contributing the most to negative water quality conditions in Fisheating Creek included cattle ranches, dairy farms, tree plantations and citrus groves. The Highlands County portion of the watershed is utilized mostly for agriculture and this is where most of the water quality issue originate. In 1998 FDEP identified Fisheating Creek as one of 25 "impaired water bodies" in the Central and South Florida regions. DEP reported that Fisheating Creek has excessive nutrients (i.e. phosphorous), low levels of dissolved oxygen and high concentrations of iron and chlorides as well as coliform bacteria, all of which are being discharged into Lake Okeechobee through Fisheating Creek. Studies of stocking rates for beef cattle have shown that reduction of cattle density does not significantly reduce phosphorous levels due to the accumulation of legacy phosphorous in the soil which has an overriding influence in surface runoff water quality. It has been suggested that a more effective strategy is to reduce runoff from cattle pastures.

The cattle industry has pro-actively addressed water quality issues. In June of 1999, after two years of effort, the Florida Cattleman's Association produced a manual entitled "Water Quality Best Management Practices for Cow/Calf Operations in Florida" for beef cattle ranches to help minimize phosphorous discharges. Guidelines include fertilization practices, erosion control, feeding and watering site adjustments and water control and storage. The Florida Department of Agriculture and Consumers Service along with the Natural Resource Conservation Service has implemented cost sharing programs to help reimburse ranchers for implementation of these Best Management Practices (BMP's).

However, BMP's are voluntary and if not economically feasible, a rancher most likely will not implement them. Currently BMP in the Fisheating Creek watershed are limited to owner funded agricultural BMP's or grant funded BMP's. Despite voluntary implementation of BMP's, phosphorous concentration levels in Lake Okeechobee have tripled since the 1960's from 30 or less parts per billion (ppb) to over 100 ppb today during periods of high rainfall and runoff. This is due to legacy phosphorous inputs into the lake from runoff and also from the bottom sediments in Lake Okeechobee which contain thousands of tons of phosphorous washed into the lake over the years and which buffers changes in total phosphorous.

In 2000 the Comprehensive Everglades Restoration Plan (CERP) was approved as part of the Water Resources Development Act of 2000. The CERP provides a framework to restore, protect, and preserve the water resources of central and Southern Florida including the Everglades. It is a 30 year program affecting 16 counties and will cost billions of dollars to implement.

The Lake Okeechobee Watershed encompasses what is now referred to as the Northern Everglades, the vast area north and west of Lake Okeechobee which forms the headwater area for the Everglades proper and is occupied by the Kissimmee River and Lake Okeechobee drainage basins. The Northern Everglades also roughly coincides with Florida's Final Frontier. For years much of the emphasis on restoring the Everglades has focused on land located south of Lake Okeechobee including the Everglades Agricultural Area. However, it is now known that much of the pollution entering the Everglades originates north of Lake Okeechobee from agricultural and urban runoff and alteration of destruction of wetlands located within the Lake Okeechobee Watershed.

Researchers have determined that Lake Okeechobee has been subjected to three long term impacts: excess phosphorous loads, unnaturally high and low water levels, and rapid spread of exotic and nuisance exotic plants. As a result of the limited progress in reducing phosphorous levels in the lake and to establish a restoration and protection program, in 2000 the Florida Legislature passed the Lake Okeechobee Protection Act (LOPA) which requires that State water quality standards be met no later than January 1, 2015. The LOPA was amended by the Legislature in 2007 to include protection and restoration of the Lake Okeechobee Watershed as well as the St. Lucie and Caloosahatchee Watersheds and was renamed the Northern Everglades and Estuaries Protection Program or NEEPP.

In 2001 per the Federal Clean Water Act, FDEP established a Total Maximum Daily Load (TMDL) standard for phosphorous entering Lake Okeechobee. TMDL is defined as "the amount of a pollutant a water body can assimilate while also remaining in compliance with State water quality standards." The TMDL established for Lake Okeechobee is 140 metric tons per year which includes 35 metric tons per year falling directly on the lake from rainfall. This would achieve an in-lake target phosphorous concentration of 40 ppb, much less than the current levels which can at times exceed 100 plus ppb. During the five year period between 2007 through 2011, the average annual amount of phosphorous entering Lake Okeechobee was 352 metric tons which is two and a half times more than the current established TMDL of 140 tons per year.

As a required component of the LOPA, the Lake Okeechobee Protection Plan (LOPP) was submitted to the Legislature in 2004 by the SFWMD, FDEP, and the Florida Department of Agriculture and Consumer Services (FDACS) and subsequently updated on February 2008 and 2011. This document is a mind numbing 463 pages and includes charts, graphs diagrams, maps and other detailed data with over one hundred acronyms.

The LOPP identified plans, schedules and costs to reduce total Phosphorus levels in Lake Okeechobee and its tributaries including Fisheating Creek. Analysis of Fisheating Creek water quality data from samples taken between 1991 and 2005 revealed that it contributed about 10.7 % of the average annual phosphorous load entering Lake Okeechobee. In addition, the average annual concentration of phosphorous in Fisheating Creek was 199 ppb or 22% higher than Lake Okeechobee's average annual concentration level of 163 ppb during that same time period. The phosphorous loads in the Fisheating Creek sub-basin are correlated with the creek's discharge rates. During low flow years the average annual phosphorous loads are also low such as in the years 2000 and 2007 when they were less than 10 metric tons. During high flow years the average annual phosphorous loads are also high such as in 1998 and 2004 when they were over 100 and 120 metric tons respectively.

The LOPP is proposing a host of measures to reduce nutrients (nitrogen and phosphorus) from entering the lake including BMP's, new regulations, and last but not least, structural solutions consisting of construction of reservoirs and storm water treatment areas (STAs) to hold and treat polluted runoff from agricultural areas within the Lake Okeechobee Watershed (which includes the Kissimmee River sub-watershed) prior to releasing the runoff into Lake Okeechobee.

Reservoirs are also proposed to capture excess runoff from Fisheating Creek for later release into Lake Okeechobee to help control water levels in the lake. A reservoir in combination with an STA has also been proposed for some sites and is termed a Reservoir Assisted Stormwater Treatment Area (RASTA). For many years Lake Okeechobee water levels have been kept abnormally high which has damaged the lakes littoral zone marshes and also caused the need to release excess water to tide through the Caloosahatchee and St. Lucie Rivers, harming both of those rivers estuaries. Offsite STA's and RASTA's will improve the lakes operating water levels to a more ecologically desirable range and avoid discharges to these estuaries. These STA's and RASTA appear to be needed, however the location of some of the proposed STA's and RASTA's within the Fisheating Creek Watershed are troubling and problematic from an environmental standpoint.

To meet the goals of the LOPA, the LOPP and the NEEPP, the Final Report of the Lake Okeechobee Watershed Construction Project Phase II Technical Plan (P2PT) was issued by the SFWMD in 2008. RASTA's were proposed at numerous sites within the Lake Okeechobee Watershed including the Fisheating Creek and Nicodemus Slough sub-watersheds.

Four different alternatives within the Fisheating Creek Watershed were presented based on the sometimes competing goals of reduction of phosphorous, maximum water storage, or a combination of the two.

Nicodemus Slough was identified in Alternative 4 (storage and water quality) as the site of the proposed 17,500 acres Nicodemus Slough RASTA which includes a reservoir to store water received from Fisheating Creek as well as high water from Lake Okeechobee before eventually discharging water back into Lake Okeechobee. The RASTA would include a 6,500 acre STA as well as an 11,000 acre, 16 foot deep reservoir. The RASTA would be in an area bounded by the Herbert Hoover Dike on the north and west, by the Seaboard Coastline Railroad on the south, and by SR 78 on the east. A majority of the RASTA would occupy lands included in the Fisheating Creek Ecosystem Florida Forever protect (also know as the Phase III optional conservation easement area in the Fisheating Creek Settlement

Agreement) consisting of the wetlands of Nicodemus Slough on the eastern third and ecologically valuable uplands including prairie habitat and numerous listed species of animals on the remaining western two thirds.

The report stated that a RASTA system was required because of the flashy nature of flood events within the basin. The reservoir would capture and store peak flows which could then be sent in sustained flows for most of the year to the STA for treatment of the runoff before discharging into Lake Okeechobee.

The report also proposed as a part of Alternative 2 (maximum storage) the 17,500 acre Fisheating Creek Reservoir within Nicodemus Slough. This reservoir would be up to 16 feet deep and would store and treat peak flows received from Fisheating Creek as well as high water from Lake Okeechobee. This would cover the same basic area as the Alternative 4 Nicodemus Slough RASTA but without the STA.

Alternative 3 (maximum water quality) recommended the Fisheating Creek RASTA II in the lower reaches of Fisheating Creek which would include a 1,350 acre 12 foot deep reservoir and a 450 acre STA. This RASTA would be located just west of Lakeport north of the Herbert Hoover Dike and south of Sixmile Marsh on primarily improved pasture lands. Alternative 3 also recommended a Fisheating Creek RASTA I in the upper headwaters of Fisheating Creek consisting of a 3,000 acre 10 foot deep reservoir and a 9,000 acre STA. This RASTA would be located adjacent to the west bank of Fisheating Creek in the vicinity of where C.R. 731 crosses the creek near Venus. Both of these RASTA's would receive flows from and discharges back into Fisheating Creek

Unfortunately, in order for Alternative II or IV RASTA's to receive water from Fisheating Creek, the plans called for construction of a relatively large water control structure within the channel of Fisheating Creek west of SR 78 in order to divert water into the RASTA'S. Reviewing agencies and environmental groups stated that this structure could impede navigation of aquatic species as well as potentially flood the lower basin and impact archaeological sites, in particular the Ft. Center Mounds as well as critical habitat including the Swallowtail kite summer Roost in Cowbone Marsh.

Many agencies provided comments to the SFWMD on the P2PT including the Nature Conservancy (TNC). In 2007 TNC provided written comments on the proposal to construct STA's on sensitive habitats throughout the Kissimmee River and Lake Okeechobee Basins including Nicodemus Slough and Fisheating Creek. TNC stated that plans to inundate these lands through water storage and/or reservoirs, including portions of the Fisheating Creek and Nicodemus Slough watersheds were of great concern to them.

TNC vigorously objected to the inundation of intact and ecologically significant habitats including dry prairie, mesic flatwoods, scrub, prairie hammocks, and wetlands. The TNC stated that any actions to improve phosphorus reduction and water storage should not degrade existing high quality upland and wetland habitats and the SFWMD should employ restoration strategies to maximize the ability of natural systems to store and clean water.

The U.S. Fish and Wildlife Service (FWS) expressed concerns as well, and commented that the proposal to inundate up to 90,000 acres of habitat within the entire Lake Okeechobee Watershed (including the Fisheating Creek sub drainage area) could have negative impacts to Audubon's crested caracara, Florida grasshopper sparrow, Swallowtail kite, eastern indigo snake and habitat for the Florida panther including proposed panther corridors. The FWS also expressed concern with the plan to create a reservoir in the lower Fisheating Creek and how that would exacerbate low water conditions by storing too much of the creek's flow. The FWS was also concerned that this reservoir would require a weir or other water control structure that would block migration of aquatic species up an down the creek corridor. The FWS recommended that the SFWMD evaluate the numerous cultural resources within the Fisheating Creek and Nicodemus Slough watersheds that would be impacted by these projects.

It appears that Nicodemus Slough may the preferred alternative however this will not be known until completion of the Final Report for the Fisheating Creek Feasibility Study originally scheduled for completion in early 2012 but still under review. This study will include the preferred plans, costs, and implementation schedules for improving water quality within the Fisheating Creek sub basin.

In 2010, at a special meeting held in Kissimmee Florida, Agricultural Secretary Kathleen Merrigan had some good news for Fisheating Creek supporters when she announced that the United States Department of Agriculture (USDA) through its Wetlands Reserve Program (WRP), will spend 89 million dollars to purchase conservation easements and restore wetlands on 26,000 acres of land located on five ranches adjacent to Fisheating Creek in Highlands County. In addition, archaeological surveys will be performed on the 26,000 acres. The purchase is one of the largest easement purchases in the history of the USDA's WRP. The four ranches where the easements have been purchased are the Westby Ranch, the

Carlton Ranch, the Clark Ranch and the Blue Head Ranch. The largest easement purchase is on the Blue Head Ranch which at 65,000 acres is by far the largest landholding in the headwaters area of Fisheating Creek and where approximately 10,000 acres will be protected by easements.

The restoration efforts will include re-flooding of altered wetlands, installation of water control structures to restore hydrology and control of exotic plants and re-establishment of native plants. The Nature Conservancy and the SFWMD partnered with the USDA in this effort. According to the spokesperson for Atlantic Blue the easements on the ranch will not affect the proposed plans for development of the property.

The WRP program was established by Congress as part of the 1990 Farm Bill. WRP is administered by the National Resources Conservation Service (NRCS) and is a voluntary program offering land owners and Tribes the opportunity to protect, restore and enhance wetlands on their property in exchange for retiring eligible land from agriculture and restoring it back to a wetland. In 2012, there were over 1.9 million acres enrolled in the WRP. The program offers three enrollment options: (1.) Permanent conservation easement in perpetuity with USDA paying 100% of the easement value and up to 100% of the restoration costs; (2.) Thirty year easement which expires after 30 years and USDA pays 75% of the easement value and up to 75% of the restoration costs; and (3.) Restoration cost-share agreement to restore or enhance without an easement and USDA pays up to 75% of the restoration costs. Fortunately, the WRP program for Fisheating Creek will utilize option one with a perpetual easement.

The WRP announcement for Fisheating Creek reflects a change in the Federal government's role in wetlands management. Surveys taken over two decades ago indicated that agricultural activities have been responsible for 80% of wetlands losses in the United States. By 1980 the criteria governing cost sharing for the Small Watershed Program also included stringent environmental constraints. In 1985 the focus began to change in Federal farm legislation that historically encouraged wetlands drainage and instead the focus began to be on use of disincentives and incentives to encourage landowners to protect and restore wetlands. The SCS Small Watershed Program no longer puts priorities on agricultural drainage projects and now the program is being directed toward water quality improvements. Although drainage projects are still authorized, in the 1990's over half of the channelization projects planned for existing projects were eliminated.

In 1990 the program was amended to provide authority to assist local governments in acquiring perpetual conservation easements on wetlands and floodplains to improve water quality, reduce flood damages, and provide habitat for fish and wildlife. Unfortunately the program seeks 50% cost sharing for wetlands easements but provides full funding for more intensive structural measures such as dams and levees and canals.

THE FLORIDA PANTHER

The Fisheating Creek Ecosystem may play a role in the eventual expansion of the Florida panther into South/Central Florida. Researchers have identified it as one of three areas north of the Caloosahatchee River that is large enough and that has suitable habitat and prey to support a small sub-population of panthers.

The Florida panther (Puma concolor coryi) is a subspecies of Puma, also referred to as as cougar, mountain lion, painter, and catamount; and is the only known population of Puma living east of the Mississippi River. Historically this subspecies ranged throughout the southeast within the states of Arkansas, Louisiana, Mississippi, Alabama, Georgia, Florida and portions of Tennessee and South Carolina. Due to persecution by humans and loss of habitat, the breeding population is now confined to South Florida south of the Caloosahatchee River and Lake Okeechobee. Current estimates are that there are between 120 and 160 animals remaining. This is a significant increase over the estimated 20 or less remaining in the early 1970's.

Until 1950, Florida panthers were unprotected and could be shot at will. In 1950, the Florida Game and Freshwater Fish Commission, now known as the Florida Fish and Wildlife Conservation Commission (FWC), acknowledged the decline of the panther and designated it as a game animal. This provided some protection by only allowing it to be hunted during an established hunting season. In 1958, the FWC gave the panther full protection and killing a panther became illegal. In 1967 the U.S. Fish and Wildlife Service (FWS) designated the panther an Endangered Species. In 1978 the Florida panther Act added another layer of protection by making it a felony to kill a panther.

By 1970 the existence of the Florida panther was in question by some. As a result, the World Wildlife Fund initiated and funded a survey of Florida panthers to determine if they still existed and if so, their numbers and locations. In 1972, 1973, and 1974, surveys were completed by houndsman and biologist Roy McBride and FWS biologist Ron Nowak. In 1972 a road killed panther was confirmed in Collier County and a female panther was captured in a bobcat trap in Collier County. In 1973 McBride and Nowak captured an old female panther near Gator Slough, a tributary to Fisheating Creek on Lykes property northeast of Palmdale and within the current boundaries of the Fisheating Creek Ecosystem project. This capture confirmed reports of a panther roaming west of Lake Okeechobee and is significantly the only female panther ever documented north of the Caloosahatchee River. All other panthers documented north of the River have been males. McBride and Nowak also confirmed evidence of two panthers in the Fakahatchee Strand in Collier County in 1974.

The World Wildlife Fund survey confirmed that panthers did indeed still exist, however the survey also concluded there were only 10 to 20 panthers remaining south of the Caloosahatchee River and that they appeared to be in poor health from inbreeding and on the brink of extinction. This knowledge set in motion efforts by local, State, and Federal Government agencies to develop a plan for recovery of the panther.

In 1981 the FWC began routinely capturing panthers and fitting them with radio collars to determine their movements, locations, natural history, and health. Between 1981 and 2004 over 70,000 locations of radio collared panthers were recorded. The process started with the use of McBride's trained dogs to track and tree a panther which was then darted. Once the tranquilizer took effect, the panther would usually topple out of the tree and be caught in a safety net or airbag to prevent injury. Occasionally a FWC biologist would have to climb the tree to help extract a tranquilized panther by lowering it down with a rope. While under the influence of the tranquilizers, the panther was weighed, measured and otherwise thoroughly inspected and blood samples were taken by the FWC biologists. And finally, a collar containing a small radio transmitter was placed on the panther. Collared panthers could then be tracked during the daytime through use of fixed winged aircraft.

In addition, through the use of swamp buggies and McBride's dogs, collared panthers were re-captured on a periodic basis to monitor their health and to replace radio batteries on their collars. The swamp buggy and dog team were also used in conjunction with hand held ground receivers to locate denning females and to find dead panthers whose transmitters emitted a different signal when there was no movement after so many minutes.

Valuable information was obtained over the years including the physical condition of the panthers, their range, preferred habitats and food, breeding areas, denning areas of females, dispersal patterns of young male panthers. Researchers identified and classified three important panthers zones in South Florida, the Primary Zone, Secondary Zones and Dispersal Zone. The Primary Zone are those areas where panthers are currently living and breeding and includes Big Cypress National Preserve (BCNP), the Florida panther National Wildlife Refuge (FPNWR), Everglades National Park (ENP) and Fakahatchee Strand State Preserve (FSSP). The Secondary Zone are those areas around the fringe of the Primary Zone currently used by few panthers and where habitat would need to be improved to be useful to panthers (i.e. Everglades Water Conservation Areas, farm lands, etc.). The Dispersal Zone is a small area which has been identified east of LaBelle where males panthers are not denning or breeding but which they have occasionally used to disperse north across the Caloosahatchee River.

Collared panthers were tracked over a vast area of public lands in South Florida including the Big Cypress Preserve, Everglades National Park, and Fakahatchee Strand State Preserve, as well as on private lands in Collier and Hendry Counties. Over time it became clear that panthers seemed to prefer forested habitats and they had a preferred area or core habitat where the majority of breeding and denning was taking place. This core area is located north of I-75 (Alligator Alley) within the Bear Island Unit of Big Cypress National Preserve (BCNP), and within the Florida panther National Wildlife Refuge (FPNWR). In addition, a core area was located south of I-75 and west of S.R. 29 within the Fakahatchee Strand State Preserve. The FPNWR and the Bear Island Unit contain more uplands and more hardwood hammocks than the Everglades or the southern BCNP and more of the prey animals that the panthers prefer including wild hog, whitetail deer, raccoon and armadillo. While the Fakahatchee Strand has more wetlands and fewer prey animals than the FPNWR and Bear Island, it does contain a large expanse of primarily forested habitat that panthers seem to prefer.

It also became clear that while a few panthers were found throughout the wetter Everglades and BCNP, these areas served mainly as dispersal areas for young male panthers but not as important breeding areas even though some panthers were breeding in these areas. Another interesting fact from the radio telemetry tracking studies was that on three separate occasions three collared male panthers had dispersed north of the Caloosahatchee River through the dispersal zone into Glades County and points beyond in search of territory and breeding females. The data showed that these panthers were swimming across the same small area of the Caloosahatchee River just east of LaBelle in Glades County.

Important findings about the health of the panther were also made from these studies. During the 1980's, the estimate was made that there were only 50 or so panthers remaining south of the Caloosahatchee River. These panthers were not in the best of health due to the low population which resulted in inbreeding and genetic defects. These genetic defects included low sperm counts, immune deficiencies, undescended testicles, fetal defects, as well as unique physical traits caused from inbreeding including a crook in the end of the tail and a cowlick in the middle of the back. The FWS concluded that the panther would probably become extinct unless a genetic restoration program was implemented.

In 1995, eight female Texas cougars were released into the South Florida panther's habitat and all have successfully bred with the Florida panthers. This appears to have subsequently reduced the genetic defects of the panther as well as helped boost the overall population which is currently (2013) estimated to be as high as 160 animals.

Researchers also concluded that the Caloosahatchee River appeared to be an impediment to panthers dispersing north.   Prior to the dredging and channelizing of the River in the early 1900's, the river didn't connect to Lake Okeechobee as it does today. The headwaters were located in lake Flirt which was just east of LaBelle and it is assumed that panthers were dispersing in and out of Southwest Florida through this gap between Lake Flirt and Lake Okeechobee. Although numerous panthers both collared and uncolored had also been documented by the FWC north of the river, all were males with the exception of the previously mentioned female captured by McBride and Nowak in 1973 near Fisheating Creek northeast of Palmdale. This meant that there were no breeding populations occurring north of the Caloosahatchee River and the panthers in South Florida were in effect an isolated population with a restricted gene pool. Land north of the Caloosahatchee River was described by biologists as a "dispersal sink" because males were dispersing there and living out their lives but not breeding.

In mid January 1988, panther tracks were spotted on the Archbold Biological Station property located in Highlands County six or seven miles south of Lake Placid and a few miles north of Venus.   After two weeks of searching, FWC biologist Jayde Roof and McBride treed the panther just east of U.S. 27 near Venus using McBride's specially trained dogs. The panther was examined and determined to be very healthy male. The panther was radio collared and designated as panther 24. panther 24 was tracked for seven months until he was discovered dead near Palmdale just east of U.S. 27 of unknown causes.   panther 24 had spent time east and north of Palmdale in the vicinity of Fisheating Creek and a tributary (Gopher Gully) but was also quite the traveler and was tracked all the way north to near Avon Park and Highlands Hammock State Park.   It is believed that numerous other panthers lived on the ranches of Highlands and Glades Counties and panther 24 proved that not enough had been done to look for them.

In 1991 the FWS issued the Florida panther Recovery Plan (The Plan) which has subsequently been revised three times. The latest (third) revision was issued in 2008. The Plan described the existing conditions of the panther and its habitat and recommended goals and objectives needed for the panther to recover with the ultimate goal of removing the panther from the endangered species list. The Plan stated that continued habitat loss and fragmentation in South Florida due to urban development, agricultural expansion (citrus, sugarcane, row crops) and roads were major threats to the panther's existence. Although the Plan noted an increasing trend in the population of panthers (current estimate of 120-160 animals) in south Florida, it also noted that there is insufficient habitat in South Florida to sustain a viable population of panthers. A viable population is defined as a population of at least 240 which can be distributed in either one contiguous area or as a meta population composed of subpopulations totaling at least 240 animals. A meta population is two or more partially isolated populations (sub-populations) which are linked by dispersal events (corridors).

The Plan sets out recovery goals for the panther that include maintenance, expansion and restoration of the panther's population and its habitat in South Florida; reintroduction of at least two viable populations within the historic range; expansion of the South Florida population into South/Central Florida; and facilitation of panther recovery through public awareness and education

The Plan also states that in order to maintain, expand and restore the panther and its habitat in South Florida, much of which is located on private lands, all levels of government must cooperate with private landowners and offer voluntary incentives to protect the panther and its habitat in the primary, secondary and dispersal zones through land acquisition, conservation easements and habitat management. That work is ongoing and on June 23, 2008 moved a step forward through the approval of the Florida panther Protection Plan (FPPP), a plan developed by a coalition of leading environmental groups and private landowners in Collier County who will attempt to assist in the recovery of the panther in Southwest Florida. The FPPP is an incentive based land use program that will attempt to insure the preservation of a contiguous corridor of private panther habitat from the Florida panther Refuge and the Big Cypress Swamp on the south with Corkscrew Swamp Sanctuary and the Okaloacoochee Slough on the north.

The FWS Panther Recovery Plan recommends the reintroduction of at least two viable populations within the panther's historic range. The FWS has identified 9 sites within the historic range of the Florida panther which may be suitable for panther reintroduction. One is located wholly within Florida within the Apalachicola National Forest, one is located partially within Florida and Georgia within the Okefenokee National Wildlife Refuge/Osceola National Forest areas, four are located within Arkansas, and one each within Louisiana, Mississippi and Alabama.

Between 1988 and 1995, 26 radio collared Texas Pumas were released in the vicinity of the Okefenokee National Wildlife Refuge in southeast Georgia and the Osceola National Forest in northeast Florida. The purpose of these releases was to determine the biological feasibility of reintroducing panther into portions of their historic range. The results of this experiment indicated that there was sufficient prey and habitat in north Florida and south Georgia to support reintroduction of a panther population outside of south Florida. However, the experiment also revealed that local landowners were lukewarm about the idea and that political and social issues will indeed require public support and education for this reintroduction to succeed.

The Panther Recovery Plan also recommends the expansion of the south Florida panther population into south/Central Florida. A study of suitable habitat was completed by the U.S. Geological Survey and the University of Tennessee, Department of Forestry, Wildlife and Fisheries and submitted to the FWS in 2003. The study area included lands from just south of Orlando all the way to Lake Okeechobee and the Caloosahatchee River. A map delineating panther habitat north of the Caloosahatchee River was created using statistical modeling in combination with Geographic Information System (GIS). Variables used to delineate this habitat included land cover, preferred panther habitat and existing development patterns, road density, and human population densities.

Four areas of contiguous panther habitat or "Habitat Patches" were identified north of the Caloosahatchee River along with potential dispersal zones or corridors between these patches. In addition, a dispersal zone was identified just east of LaBelle connecting the south Florida population with the four habitat patches to the north. The four habitat patches identified north of the Caloosahatchee River are referred to as the Avon Park Bombing Range; Duette Park/Manatee County; Eastern Fisheating Creek; and Babcock-Webb Wildlife Management Area/Fisheating Creek.

The Eastern Fisheating Creek, and Babcock-Webb Wildlife Management Area/Fisheating Creek patches were discussed together. This habitat patch is separated by U.S. 27 and encompasses 679 square miles, larger than either the Avon Park or Duette Park/Manatee County habitat patches at 599 and 408 square miles respectively. It is comprised of lands located in Glades County, southeast Highlands County and eastern Charlotte County. This habitat patch is located closest to the existing panther habitat south of the Caloosahatchee River. The habitat study stated that only two publicly owned parcels are located within this habitat patch, Cecil Webb WMA and portions of Fisheating Creek protected by fee simple ownership and conservation easements. The study failed, however, to account for the subsequent State purchased Babcock Ranch in Charlotte County which adds another 115 square miles of public land within this habitat patch.

Of the four habitat patches identified north of the Caloosahatchee River, it is estimated that Avon Park can support 10-12 panthers, the Babcock-Webb-Fisheating Creek habitat patch can support 14-16 panthers and the Duette Park/Manatee County may be able to support 8 panthers. This is a relatively small subpopulation of panthers scattered over a wide area and researchers are concerned that maintaining a social structure may be problematic. Males would have to disperse long distance and cross some major roadways in order to breed with females. It would only take the loss of a few animals to disrupt the social structure of the entire population and the end result could be the loss of all panthers north of the Caloosahatchee River.

As mentioned, researchers have identified a south Florida dispersal zone which connects the Okaloacoochee Slough on the south with a crossing on the Caloosahatchee River on the north just east of LaBelle. Radio telemetry data show the river crossing point has been used at three separate times by three radio collared males since 1988. North of the river crossing, in Glades County researchers have identified a large private ranch with habitats that may be suitable for panthers. The importance of this connection cannot be overstated. According to the late biologist David Maher "the ultimate wildlife mitigation for South Florida would be to physically reunite the known range of the panthers in South Florida with the forests of Charlotte, Glades, and Highlands Counties in South/Central Florida." He suggested an overpass across the River similar to landscaped land bridges for wildlife which have been built across at least two Florida Interstates. Since the Caloosahatchee River is part of the Okeechobee Waterway and is used not only by recreational boats, including sailboats, but also by industrial barges, I believe this may not be a feasible solution, however preservation of the dispersal area would be an important first step and development from LaBelle is quickly encroaching on this important dispersal area.

Researchers have stated that the river itself is not an impediment to panthers crossing since they are known to be excellent swimmers and regularly cross rivers much larger in the western United States. However the combination of the river, as well as S.R 80 just south of the river, along with incompatible land uses may be what is discouraging more panthers, especially females, from crossing there. Perhaps the use of fencing and construction of an underpass on S.R. 80 along with enhancements to the landscape within the dispersal area could make this a viable corridor. This dispersal zone is the only one of the four identified that does not require panthers to cross a major highway such as an Interstate, an important consideration because past studies of radio-collared females showed very few crossed major highways and major highways often formed boundaries of both male and females panthers home ranges. However, the habitat study also noted that extensive agricultural lands and urban development near LaBelle and Lehigh Acres could inhibit use of this dispersal zone.

Recognizing the importance of the South Florida dispersal zone, in 1998 the State of Florida delineated 18,455 acres within the dispersal zone and added it to the Florida Forever project list as the "Caloosahatchee Ecoscape" project. Up until 2012, only about 4,940 acres had been protected within the project boundary through purchase of a conservation easement on the LaBelle Ranch located at the south end of the project boundary and through creation of a 4,000 acre panther conservation bank in the middle of the project area. In 2008, the Caloosahatchee Ecoscape project was moved to the Group A list which are those projects with the highest priority for purchase.

Interestingly, the eastern boundary of this Florida Forever project is an abandoned railroad grade which researchers believe may facilitate its use as a dispersal corridor. The southern boundary stops just north of the Okaloachoochee Slough State Forest. The western boundary of this project abuts the outskirts of the growing Town of LaBelle and the abutting lands are designated as Residential on the Hendry County Future Land Use Map. Hendry County is in the direct path of the growth expanding eastward from Ft. Myers and Lehigh Acres. The Glades County Future Land Use Map has designated lands directly north of the dispersal area across the Caloosahatchee River as Agriculture along with some small areas of residential, commercial and transitional land uses associated with the small community of Ortona.

In 2012 there was some good news for this project with the announcement that a 1,278 acre conservation easement had been purchase on the critical area located between SR 80 on the south and the Caloosahatchee River on the north within the project area. The easement protects over a mile and a half of river frontage on the north side of SR 80. The new owner of this property has named it the Lone Ranger Forge and agreed to sell the easement to the TNC. This was a cooperative effort with many partners including the landowner; The Florida Chapter of The Nature Conservancy, who also managed the transaction and its closing; the FWS; the US Department of Agriculture Wetlands Reserve Program; the US Army Corps of Engineers; the National Fish and Wildlife Foundation and Walmart. A conservation easement was acquired on part of the project where ranching activities will continue and another easement was acquired on the wetland portion of the project where wetland restoration and enhancement will occur. The TNC and Natural Resources Conservation Service will manage the easements.

This easement is a step in the right direction, however many acres still need to be protected within the project area to ensure the existence of this critical dispersal corridor for the Florida panther. The critical nature of this project can be seen upon viewing a Google aerial of the project where residential growth from LaBelle can be seen encroaching from the west including a large subdivision which wraps around the west and northwest sides of the recently purchased Lone Ranger Ranch easements. Time is running out to protect the dispersal zone lands within the Caloosahatchee Ecoscape. Hopefully, with cooperation from the landowners within this project area, the remaining lands can be protected through either outright purchase or though purchase of conservation easements. Researchers note that if panthers populations continue to expand, this dispersal zone will play a key role in maintaining a corridor connection between existing panther habitat in South Florida and potential habitats to the north should a meta population become established there.

Since 1972 male panthers from South Florida have been documented in south/Central Florida 19 times. Researchers believe these are all males dispersing from the south Florida population and that there is an increase in males dispersing across the Caloosahatchee River into south/Central Florida due to the corresponding increase in the breeding population south of the Caloosahatchee River. The lack of any female panthers in South/Central Florida has prevented the expansion of panthers there. Ideally, researchers hope that if the Caloosahatchee Ecoscape dispersal zone can be preserved, both male and female panthers will disperse north and south thus creating gene flow in and out of the existing South Florida habitat area.

The FWS Recovery Plan states that female panthers have short dispersal distances and human intervention will likely be required to establish female panthers in Central Florida. Researchers have noted that male panthers captured north of the Caloosahatchee River have all appeared to be in good condition which indicates there is an adequate prey and cover to support the species. There is no doubt that establishing a breeding population within South Central Florida is going to be problematic but hopefully with the cooperation of private landowners through government incentives as well as the support of the citizens of Florida, the panther can have a future there as well as in South Florida.

The Panther Recovery Plans calls for facilitation of panther recovery through public awareness and education. This program includes education material for residents living in and adjacent to panther habitat, and information for livestock owners to help minimize panther depredation including establishment of a depredation fund. Fortunately for the Florida panther, unlike their western cousins, there has never been a documented case of an attack on a human. According to the late biologist David Meahr, panthers appear to prefer wild prey over domestic animals and he was not aware of any ranchers who had experienced cattle depredation on a regular basis. However, as urban growth from the Southwest Florida coast has steadily infringed on panther habitat, human panther conflicts have increased. Over a four and a half year period between December 2003 and June 2007, there were 16 incidents of depredation of domestic livestock and/or attacks on pets.

A recent development in tracking technology has provided some new information about the panther's habitat preferences. Since 1981, researchers have used VHF technology to monitor panthers. Panthers were monitored with fixed wing aircraft three times per week and only during the morning hours thus obtaining only diurnal (daytime) habitat data. The thought occurred that since panthers are nocturnal and most active during the period just before dark to just after sunrise, the VHF data was biased towards habitat selection only during daylight hours and thus was insufficient for showing nocturnal habitat preference. This realization was importance because habitat use is used in reviewing the potential impacts to panthers from proposed development. In addition, habitat use data is used to determine areas where panther habitat should be preserved.

It occurred to the FWC that if GPS units were used to monitor panthers, panther movement could be recorded 24 hours per day rather than the normal morning hours for VHF monitoring. The FWC decided to conduct a special study of panther movement and habitat selection using both VHF and GPS to see if the data showed different results. Between 2002-2007, the FWC conducted studies on the movement and habitat selection of 11 panthers using GPS telemetry and VHF radio telemetry. The results of the study supported earlier assumptions that forested habitats are the preferred habitats of panthers. However, the GPS study of nocturnal habitat use revealed that panthers did not avoid open wetlands/freshwater marsh habitat at night as they do during the daytime. Additionally, the GPS study showed significantly more use of open non-forested habitat consisting of dry prairie and grassland and conversely less use of forested habitat use during nocturnal periods than did the VHF data.

Researchers have previously stated that panther habitat in South Central Florida is fragmented and void of large contiguous expanses of forest. This new GPS data showing that panthers use marshes, grasslands and dry prairies at night more than previously thought may provide support to the plan to expand panthers into South Central Florida. Much of the South Central Florida habitat including that of the Babcock-Webb-Fisheating Creek habitat patch consists of open areas such as marshes, improved pasture, grasslands and dry prairie (saw palmetto flats). This is an interesting development and FWC has recommended further analysis of this information.

In 2010, the FWS announced that it will consider a request by environmental groups, including Florida Audubon and the Florida Wildlife Federation, to expand the Florida panther National Wildlife Refuge. A survey of willing sellers has identified 40,000 to 50,000 acres of land potentially available to expand the refuge. This may be problematic however, because the FWS has recently been under the microscope and some have questioned how committed the agency really is to saving the Florida panther.

The FWS has been criticized over the years for never having recommended denial of a development permit for any project proposed within known panther habitat in Southwest Florida. And beginning in 2004, former FWS employees revealed that superiors in the agency have often put pressure on staff reviewers to make recommendations of approval of developments in panther habitat out of fear that the agency would have their budgets cut as a result of pressure from the development community. One reviewer who became a whistle blower was re-assigned out of the panther recovery program. Some FWS staffers have stated that unfortunately the FWS has unofficially written off the Florida panther but will not say that in public.

THE FLORIDA BLACK BEAR

The Florida black bear is a unique sub-species of the American black bear which inhabits extreme south Georgia and Alabama as well as scattered areas throughout Florida. In Florida, black bears were once found throughout the state from the panhandle all the way to the upper Florida Keys. Early settlers even reported black bears on the beaches of Florida's east coast feeding on turtle eggs. Today, according to the FWC the black bear is restricted to approximately 17% of its former range. The FWC recognizes six core populations and two remnant or sub-populations. The six core populations are located at Eglin Air Force base in the panhandle; the Apalachicola National Forest southwest of Tallahassee; the Osceola National Forest west of Jacksonville; the Ocala National Forest north of Orlando; the St. Johns River population located east of the St. Johns River in northern Volusia County; and the Big Cypress National Preserve east of Naples. The two remnant populations are found in the Chassahowitzka National Wildlife Refuge north of Tampa and in northern Glades County/southern Highlands County, south of Lake Placid. Researchers believe the core populations are viable and stable and may even be increasing in population but that the two remnant populations face an uncertain future due to their small isolated population coupled with habitat loss and encroaching development.

Prior to 1950 the black bear was unprotected and could be hunted or killed year round in Florida. In 1950 the black bear was designated as a game animal by the FWC with legal hunting seasons running concurrently with the deer season. In 1971 bear hunting was restricted only to the Baker and Columbia Counties and a few wildlife management areas. In 1974 the black bear was designated as a threatened species except in Baker and Columbia Counties and the Apalachicola National Forest where they could still be legally hunted during the fall hunting season. In 1994 the FWC decided to ban hunting of Florida black bear. In 1998 the statewide population of black bears was determined by the FWC to be approximately 1,282. Currently the FWC estimates that there are between 2,500 and 3,000 bears in Florida.

The Glades/Highlands sub-population of black bear covers a core area of approximately 50,000 acres or 78 square miles in northern Glades County, including a portion of the Fisheating Creek Ecosystem, and in southern Highlands County. This sub-population consists of approximately 100 to 150 bears. The secondary area surrounding the core area runs south to the Caloosahatchee River and north to Lake Kissimmee. U.S. 27 runs down the center of the core area along the Lake Wells Ridge.

This population of black bears has been studied for many years by the Archbold Biological Station located in southern Highlands County and by the FWC and more recently (since 2003) by the University of Kentucky (UK). The UK researchers have captured, collared and tracked over 50 black bears in the Glades/Highlands population since 2004 as part of a black bear ecology and conservation study. As with the Florida panther, before attempting to develop a plan to save this isolated species, information must be gathered on its annual and seasonal habitat use, its distribution within the core and secondary areas, and its potential for dispersal within the Glades/Highlands region as well as to outlying populations especially the Big Cypress population to the south across the Caloosahatchee River.

Bears tracked with radio collars and GPS by the UK since 2004 have provided valuable information on their movements and distribution. Tracking maps identified bears using habitat from the west side of Lake Istokpoga and south all the way to Ortona north of La Belle. Clusters of habitat being used by this sub-population of black bear were also identified at the Royce Ranch (Lake Wales Ridge Wildlife and Environmental Area) located on the west side of Lake Istokpoga; within the Archbold Biological Station property; within the Smoak Grove, Hendrie and Lightsey XL Ranches in Highlands County; north of Ortona; and within the Fisheating Creek Ecosystem especially Cowbone Marsh, Gopher Gully and Gator Slough.

The dense but fragmented bay swamps or baygall swamps are found on the east edge of the Lake Wales Ridge east of U.S. 27 from Lake Istokpoga southward. These swamps appear to be favored by the bears for cover and as denning sites and were used more often than any other type of cover followed secondly by the xeric scrub on the Lake Wales Ridge where the bears forage for acorns and other mast. The baygall swamps grow in a peat substrate that is usually saturated and where fire is rare or non-existent and consists of a closed canopy of evergreen trees including loblolly bay, sweetbay, swamp bay, titi, and fetterbush. Florida black bears have an average home range of 14 square miles for females and 62 square miles for males. Unlike the Florida panthers, they are not particularly territorial and overlaps in their home ranges are tolerated. They are mostly solitary except for females with cubs.

Young males between the ages of 2 to 4 will disperse to other territories due to pressure from other adult males or to find a mate. Researcher believe the average dispersal distance for young males is approximately 37 miles. Subadult females usually stay in the immediate area of their mothers home range. They are mostly vegetarian but will eat meat on occasion including

78

armadillo, wild hog, deer fawns, etc. They do not hibernate per se but will become more sedentary during the cold months of the winter and go into a semi-hibernation state of reduced activity know as winter denning or winter lethargy. Winter lethargy can be brought on by many factors including reproductive status, food availability, amount of daylight, referred to as photo-period, and temperature changes. Male bears may have a reduced denning period or no denning at all.

A 2004 a U.F. Masters Thesis on the genetics of Florida black bears by Jeremy Dixon analyzed DNA from hair and tissue samples from 305 different bears throughout Florida within nine separate populations in order to determine the genetic variation within each population. Within the Glades/Highlands sub-population, 27 bears were sampled. The analysis revealed that the Glades/Highlands sub-population of bears was second only to the Chassahowitzka population in having the lowest gene variation due to isolation from other bear populations and that both populations have been isolated longer than any of the nine populations where samples were taken in the State.

Although inbreeding signs were not seen in this sub-population, researchers believe the results of this low genetic variation could result over time in reduced fitness and survival, reduced evolutionary potential and ultimately extinction. Management recommendations included the increase in the population to at least 200 and the elimination of habitat loss and fragmentation. The study also recommended the gene flow into the Glades/Highlands population of bears be increased to historic levels through either connecting to other populations or through translocation or relocating captured bears from other populations into this sub-population.

One radio-collared bear in particular demonstrated the feasibility of connecting disjunct populations of bears through a system of corridors. The bear traveled from Collier County north all the way to Lake Placid, a distance of approximately 87 miles in 25 days, or an average of three and a half miles per day. To date, this is the longest known distance traveled by a black bear in Florida. This bear was captured by the FWC in 1986 northeast of Naples within the Golden Gate Estates development after a landowner complained that some of his chickens had been stolen by a bear. After the bear was anesthetized, he was measured and tattooed and an ear tag and radio collar were attached by FWC biologists.

The bear was radio-tracked every other day by fixed wing aircraft as well as ground triangulation. This two and a half year old male bear was located 71 times between May 4 and July 28, 1986. From May 4 to June 7 he moved within an area of approximately 12 square miles just east of where he was captured. On June 7 he began his long journey, heading northwest crossing through the Corkscrew Swamp Sanctuary, then north across S.R. 82, where he stayed in the Lehigh Acres development for 7 or 8 days. He continued north crossing busy S.R. 80 before swimming across the Caloosahatchee River, crossing through Telegraph Swamp within Babcock Ranch, then he headed northeast eventually crossing S.R. 74 and across Fisheating Creek north of Venus where he began traveling through pastures until reaching the west side of Lake Placid on July 2, 1986. From July 3 to July 28 he remained in the Lake Placid area where he traversed bay swamps, sandpine scrub, flatwoods as well as suburbs. He also raided several chicken and turkey pens and some bee hives.

Interestingly he was observed within 200 meters from a large family picnic which included use of fireworks but he appeared unconcerned and was never detected by the picnickers. Unfortunately he also did not seem to fear people so out of caution the FWC felt they had to euthanize him which was done on July 28. An autopsy revealed he had been recently shot twice and buckshot was found in his back and kidney, which was severely damaged by the gunshot.

The FWC concluded that this bear exhibited breeding season wanderings common to young males in the summer breeding season. A smaller set of bear tracks were observed alongside his tracks on several occasions in the Lake Placid area which was most likely a female. This bear also demonstrated the feasibility of maintaining or creating corridors to connect isolated bear populations such as the Glades/Highlands population with larger more intact populations such as the Big Cypress population where he started his journey. The FWC also concluded that corridors need not be well defined as long as they do not impede movements of the bears using them.

Another tracked bear, known as bear M-19, also traveled a significant distance after being captured and collared in 2007 in Highlands County. This young male began a dispersal event a few weeks after his collaring and in three months time he traveled over 1,218 miles or an impressive 8.37 miles per day on average. A data map of bear M-19's locations during this three month journey shows he headed south from Highlands County and traversed most of the Fisheating Creek Ecosystem both east and west of U.S. 27 including most of the creek corridor west of U.S. 27; southeast as far as Cowbone Marsh; northeast as far as Smoak Groves and Hendrie Ranches; northwest up Rainey Slough; and southwest through the Babcock Ranch passing through the north end of Telegraph Swamp, then traversing the west side of Telegraph Swamp, then crossing back through the south end of Telegraph Swamp before heading northeast back to Fisheating Creek.

The updated Strategic Habitat Conservation Areas (SHCA) maps produced as part of the 2009 addendum to the 1995 Gaps Report added several SHCA areas for black bear in the Glades and Highlands County where no SHCA areas were shown in the 1995 Gaps Report.   Within Highlands County SHCA areas are shown in the vicinity of the Hendrie Ranch, Smoak Groves Ranch and directly south and adjacent to Smoak Groves Ranch within the Fisheating Creek Ecosystem.   A small SHCA is shown at the headwaters of Nicodemus Slough immediately south of the Herbert Hoover Dike just east of Palmdale.   A large SHCA area is shown south of Palmdale bounded by S.R. 29 on the west, U.S. 27 on the north and east, and S.R. 78 on the south. A small SHCA area is shown adjacent to both sides of Fisheating Creek between C.R. 731 on the north and the Glades/Highlands County line on the south and another small SHCA area is shown just southeast of this SHCA within Glades County east of Fisheating Creek.

The 2009 Gaps addendum provides a sobering statistic regarding the black bear in Florida, predicting the State will lose 2.47 million acres of black bear habitat by the year 2060.

PRAIRIE BIRDS

In discussing important habitats, the GAPS report includes a section on "Prairie Birds" which discusses birds associated with the dry prairie habitats found in south and Central Florida. Birds in this group include the Florida sandhill crane, short-tailed hawk, Southern bald eagle, Florida grasshopper sparrow, Florida scrub jay, American swallowtail kite, Audubon's crested caracara, limpkin, Florida mottled duck, and Florida burrowing owl.

Because most of these birds are rare, the dry prairie, and its associated depression marshes, wet prairies, and cabbage palm hammocks, is one of the most important wildlife habitats remaining in Florida. The prairie birds are one of the least represented species on existing conservation lands. In describing areas where these rare prairie species may be found in high and diverse numbers, the report identifies lands west of Lake Okeechobee and most of central and northern Glades County. Significantly, dry prairie comprises approximately 30% or 43,000 acres of the habitat within the Fisheating Creek Ecosystem Florida Forever project boundary.

Crested Caracara

To me, no other bird is more symbolic of Central Florida's dry prairies as the Audubon's crested caracara which is endemic to this declining habitat. The Fisheating Creek Ecosystem provides large areas of improved pasture and dry prairie which provide breeding, nesting, foraging, and possibly gathering areas for the caracara. A map of listed species occurrence records from the Florida Natural Areas Inventory (FNAI) reveal that the caracara inhabits much of the Fisheating Creek Ecosystem.

Historically the caracara was common from northern Brevard County south to Hendry County but it has also been reported as far north as Nassau County in northern Florida and as far south as the Florida Keys. However, the caracara has been in decline since the early 1900's due to conversion of its native prairie to agriculture (citrus, sugarcane, improved pasture) and urban development. Researchers believe as much as 88% of the original native prairie in Central Florida has been converted into other uses, historically for improved pasture for cattle but more recently for urban development and citrus. The first recorded account of this species was in 1831 by John James Audubon who shot one near St. Augustine in order to identify it. Unfortunately, during that time, this was the common method used to identify and describe new species due to the lack of high power optics or photography.

Today the core area for the caracara is found primarily on private ranches north and west of Lake Okeechobee in Glades, Desoto, Highlands, Okeechobee and Osceola counties. Cattle ranching has converted many areas of native prairie into improved pasture but the caracara has adapted to these habitats and ranching is usually compatible with the caracara. Researchers believe that the short grasses typically found within improved pastures may help the foraging caracara find prey which is more easily seen. In addition, researchers believe that caracara benefit from prescribed burning, plowing, and mowing associated with improved pasture management practices. The only other areas in the United States where the bird can be found are in south Texas and southwestern Arizona. Its range also extends through Mexico, Central America and Cuba.

The caracara, like the bald eagle, is a unique raptor/scavenger meaning it will catch live prey as well as feed on carrion. Caracara are opportunistic feeders and will eat a variety of animals including insects such as beetles and grasshoppers, worms, maggots, snakes, rabbits, skunks, opossums, rats, mice, squirrels, lizards, young alligators, crabs, crayfish, fish, young birds, and cattle egrets. They will also regularly search along highways for road kill. Caracara will mate for life and their nesting season is typically from November through April with the peak in January and February. They typically construct their nests in the tops of cabbage palms found singly or in clumps (hammocks) within open pastures. Occasionally they will use a live oak, cypress, Australian pine, or black gum tree for their nest. Although breeding and nesting can occur in what little native prairie still existing, most of the breeding and nesting areas are now found on improved pastures located on private ranch lands.

Young caracara are known to be nomadic and recent observations and telemetry monitoring indicate that there are three large areas of improved pasture where juvenile caracara congregate during their first year. These areas are located along the Kissimmee River north of S.R. 98 (the largest of the three); one is in northern Okeechobee County; and the other is north of U.S. 27 in Glades County. However, the Glades County site may have been destroyed by conversion from pasture to sugarcane in 1997-98.

The population of the caracara is not known with certainty, due to their concentrations on inaccessible private lands, however current estimates place them at 500 or more. Based on long term surveys the population is believed to be in decline and in 1987 the U.S. Fish and Wildlife Service listed the caracara as Federally threatened. Research has shown that road mortalities are a significant source of caracara decline due to their penchant for feeding on road kill. However, habitat loss is the main reason for their decline and within the last fifteen years urban growth has sprawled south into inland areas of Central Florida formally dominated by large cattle ranches. Many researchers now believe this sprawling urban development is the single greatest threat to the caracara.

In 1989 the FWS issued its first recovery plan for the caracara. In 1999 the plan was updated as part of the Multi-Species Recovery Plan for South Florida. The objective of the recovery plan is to de-list the caracara once the recovery criteria have been met including halting the loss and fragmentation of habitat, increasing the number of territories from 200 to 300 in the core areas, increasing breeding pairs and overall population, and protection of habitat through either acquisition, conservation easements or cooperative landowner agreements. Most of the known caracara habitat is on private ranch lands so the FWS recovery plan includes recommendations to provide landowners with monetary or tax incentives to encourage lower intensity farming operations and/or preservation of native habitats in areas occupied by caracara.

As part of the recovery plan, the FWS has drafted Conservation Guidelines to protect the nests and nesting pairs of caracara. These guidelines were modeled after those established for the bald eagle with criteria for protection of primary and secondary zones around known nests. The draft also contains land management guidelines for protection of gathering or communal areas for young caracara including limiting habitat conversion to pasture and wetland habitats which would adversely affect caracara's. The plan also recommends that public lands with known caracara populations develop management plans that will protect, maintain and enhance known habitats. To date, the only publicly owned areas with known caracara populations are Avon Park Bombing Range, Kissimmee State Preserve, Three Lakes WMA and Fisheating Creek WMA.

The Management Plan for the Fisheating Creek WMA includes objectives to manage habitats for listed species including the caracara by implementing resource management guidelines consistent with State and Federal guidelines. The Management Policy Statement for the Fisheating Creek Ecosystem Florida Forever project calls for maintaining and possibly improving the status of rare plant and animal communities in order to protect rare and endangered animals that inhabit these areas.

Florida Grasshopper Sparrow

Another bird dependent upon Central Florida's dry prairies is the Florida grasshopper sparrow which is endemic to this habitat. The Fisheating Creek

Ecosystem provides large areas of improved pasture and dry prairie which may provide breeding, nesting, and foraging areas for the sparrow if properly managed with periodic burning. Burning will prevent the invasion of pines and hardwood tress into their prairie habitat. In addition, summer burns have been shown to increase the length of the breeding season. Listed species occurrence records from the Florida Natural Areas Inventory (FNAI) document the existence of the Grasshopper Sparrow on the Fisheating Creek Ecosystem.

As with the caracara, the sparrow has been in decline since the early 1900's due to conversion of its native prairie to agriculture (citrus, sugarcane, improved pasture) and urban development. The Florida grasshopper sparrow is a subspecies of the Grasshopper sparrow and the original extent of the sub-species is not know but there are early records of it from Collier and Dade Counties in the south and as far north as Osceola County. Sparrows have also been documented breeding in overgrown pastures but have abandoned these once they were cut or grazed.

Breeding populations are known from only six locations within two sub-populations of sparrows found on Three Lakes WMA and Kissimmee Prairie Preserve State Park. These are the only two areas that meet the current FWS criteria for recovery. Sparrows are also present in small numbers on Avon Park Air Force Range and the Audubon Kissimmee Prairie Sanctuary.

Researchers have identified the habitats that sparrows prefer from surveys of known breeding populations. Sparrows prefer habitats with enough open areas for foraging, approximately 22 to 36 percent, as well as enough cover for hiding from predators and for nesting. Sparrows prefer large unfragmented expanses of flat treeless grasslands composed of primarily saw palmetto and dwarf oak, along with bluestem grasses such as broomsedge, wiregrass and St. Johns Wort.

Research of sparrows in the Kissimmee Prairie found that their diet consisted of 61% animal matter (insects and spiders) and 39% plant matter (seeds and grass). Their nesting season is typically from April through June. The population of the sparrow is estimated to be less than 600. Based on long term surveys the population is believed to be in decline and in 1986 the FWS listed the sparrow as federally Endangered. Habitat loss primarily from conversion of native dry prairie to agriculture and improved pasture is the main reason for the decline.

In 1988 the FWS issued its first recovery plan for the sparrow. In 1999 the plan was updated as part of the Multi-Species Recovery Plan for South Florida. The objective of the recovery plan is to de-list the sparrow once the recovery criteria have been met including halting the loss and fragmentation of existing habitat within the Kissimmee River Basin; establishment of at least ten sites within the historic range, each containing 50 to 100 breeding pairs of sparrows; and increasing the population at each of these ten sites. Other criteria include determining the distribution and abundance of sparrows; reintroduction of sparrows into suitable habitat; development of a captive propagation plan for the sparrow; development of a landowner public awareness program; protection and enhancement of currently occupied habitat; protection and enhancement of habitat on public lands; creation, restoration and expansion of habitat; and continued research on sparrow/habitat interactions.

The FWS Recovery Plan seemed to emphasize the existing sparrow population within the Kissimmee River basin. However, in 1995 researchers flew six aerial surveys to determine where remaining suitable sparrow habitat was located. The survey results revealed that only Osceola, Desoto, and Glades Counties had large prairies containing native vegetation. Within Glades County there was a large area of marginal habitat on Lykes property on the western side of the County, and a large contiguous area of high quality habitat located on the Smoak Groves Ranch also known as the Venus Ranch. Fortunately, the Venus Ranch now has a conservation easement and is part of the Fisheating Creek Ecosystem. The report concluded that conservation of dry prairie habitat should be a top priority in these three Counties.

In addition, in 2007, researchers published a paper on the distribution, abundance, and habitat availability of the Florida grasshopper sparrow. One of their conclusions was that the large areas of protected potential habitat in Manatee, Desoto and Glades counties offer the best opportunities to meet the FWS Recovery goals for the establishment of additional sub-populations of the Florida grasshopper sparrow. Protection of the Fisheating Creek Ecosystem will help to meet these goals.

Swallowtail Kite

The northern species of the swallowtail kite is a large bird of prey which breeds in Florida and six other southeastern states. Up until the early 1900's, the kite was know to nest in at least 21 states, however, habitat destruction/alteration and possibly shooting have restricted them to their current range. Currently, researchers estimate the U.S. breeding population to number somewhere between 3,500 and 5,000 birds, two thirds of which are estimated to be in Florida.

Remarkably, the largest know aggregation of kites in North America is found on the Fisheating Creek Wildlife Management Area in the vicinity of Cowbone Marsh west of Lake Okeechobee. Between 1,350 and 2,200 kites have been recorded at this pre-migration roost site during its peak use in late July. This large roost is a communal night roost used by swallowtail kites prior to migrating 5,000 miles south where they spend the winter in South America. Researchers believe most of the kites that use this roost arrive from other nests sites in Florida, particularly Central and South Florida.

About ten miles east of U.S. 27, the cypress dominated floodplain swamp associated with Fisheating Creek abruptly transitions into a large 2,400 acre freshwater marsh know as Cowbone Marsh which then transitions into a large floodplain marsh west of S.R. 78 where it ultimately transitions into the vast marshes located on the west side of Lake Okeechobee. Biologists believe this juxtaposition of swamp and marshlands is what seems to attract the kites as the swamps offers roosting trees and the marshes offers the abundant insects which the migrating kites forage on.

The current roost site is located within a stand of dead live oaks just north of the Herbert Hoover Dike immediately south of Cowbone Marsh but researchers believe that the original roost site was located within a small isolated stand of cypress trees within the western end of Cowbone Marsh. Researchers believe that sometime during the summer of 1987, airboat activity in Cowbone Marsh caused the kites to relocate southeast to a stand of Australian Pines on Herbert Hoover Dike where they remained until 2004 when they again relocated a few hundred yards north to their current roost site.

The concentration of kites at Fisheating Creek were recorded as early as 1929 by noted South Carolina Ornithologist Alexander Sprunt Jr. as reported in his 1954 book, "Florida Bird Life." In 1987, FWC biologist Brian A. Milsap published an account of the roost in Florida Field Naturalist where he speculated that the roost may be a staging area used by the kites to build up their fat reserves prior to migrating to South America. Milsap monitored the flight patterns and numbers of these kites from July 26 to September 3, 1986. He noted that the kites would arrive in February and March and depart between June and August. He also noted that they would leave the roost in the morning and return in the afternoon but did not remark on this other than to say that they appeared to be coming from and going to the west side of Lake Okeechobee. Subsequent studies indicate that the kites leave the roost in the morning to forage in the marshes on the west side of Lake Okeechobee and return in the afternoon to the roost.

On the morning of August 7, 1987 Milsap counted 1,339 kites leaving the roost and speculated that this was at least 50% of the total kite population in the United States. At its peak in 1992 and 1993 the Fisheating Creek roost contained 2,200 kites or almost half the United States population at that time.

The Avian Research and Conservation Institute (ARCI) in Gainesville, Florida has studied the swallowtail kite for many years and provided valuable additional data since Milsap's 1987 publication. The ARCI has also provided management guidelines to the FWC for the Fisheating Creek roost. To gain a perspective on the large number of kites using the Fisheating Creek roost, the next largest pre-migration roost site is in Corkscrew Swamp Sanctuary east of Naples where a peak pre-migration roost population was documented by Milsap in 1989 of 344 birds. The third largest pre-migration roost was identified by ARCI within the upper St. Johns River basin (Jane Green Swamp) west of Melbourne with peaks of over 100 birds.

In 1996 the ARCI began tracking the migration of kites in Florida using small satellite telemetry receivers. Kites from other Florida nest sites were tracked to the Fisheating Creek roost where they then migrated to South America. The preferred route of the kites was an open water crossing across the Florida Straits to the Yucatan Peninsula. Some kites, particularly when weather was an issue, would stop briefly in western Cuba where they would rest and forage. From Yucatan, after another period of resting and foraging, they would fly south along the east side of Central America to Columbia where they crossed over the Andes Mountains and head southeast to winter in southwest Brazil, eastern Paraguay and Bolivia. The most hazardous part of their journey appears to have been the long open water crossings of the Gulf of Mexico particularly for young kites. The average time to migrate from Southern Florida to Brazil, Paraguay and Bolivia is 80 days and they appear to feed primarily on insects during their migration.

The FWC reports that the loss and degradation of critical habitats in south central and southwestern Florida where most of the remaining kites nest and roost on private lands, jeopardizes the U.S. population and has recommended the kite for listing as Endangered.

In 2007 the FWC published a report by ARCI of the threats and management options for the kite roost at Fisheating Creek. The report identified numerous threats to the kite roost and suggested potential relocation sites where the roost would be safer. The three most likely threats identified by ARCI include levee and canal maintenance associated with the Herbert Hoover Dike (located a few hundred yards south of the current roost), intrusions by birders/photographers, and disturbance by low flying aircraft.

The Herbert Hoover Dike just south of the current nest, is owned by Lykes and is used by their employees for access to their adjacent lands. In addition, the Army Corps. Of Engineers (COE) holds an easement from Lykes on that section of levee to perform maintenance. In 2005 Lykes requested that ARCI provide them with guidelines for avoiding impacts to the kites during the roosting season. These guidelines were provided and are now used by Lykes employees and COE personnel.

Of the three most likely threats, the ARCI has identified intrusions by birders as well as filmmakers and photographers as the most potentially harmful to the roost site. In July of 2006 during the peak of roosting activity, a group of birders hiked along the Herbert Hoover Dike to the roost site on public lands of the Fisheating Creek Wildlife Management Area and took photographs which were then posted on the internet along with a discussion of their trip. The FWC acted quickly and posted a 500 perimeter buffer around the roost site and declared it a biologically sensitive area with no public access. In addition, Lykes cooperated by increasing their security of the Herbert Hoover Dike to try and minimize illegal access to the roost site. ARCI has recommended establishing a kite viewing area east of the roost possibly along S.R. 78 where birders can watch them on their daily foraging flights to and from the marshes of western Lake Okeechobee. This would provide the public with views of the kites without risking disturbance to the roost.

Regarding the threat from low flying aircraft, the ARCI recommended that FWC consider requesting the FAA designate a seasonal no flight zone around the lower Fisheating Creek area without drawing attention to the specific location of the roost site.

The FWC has determined that threats to the current roost site from air boaters have now been minimized with establishment of a 2.5 kilometer "no airboat buffer" around the roost implemented by the Fisheating Creek Management Plan.

Ironically the current roost site was created by the application of herbicides to an adjacent stand of Australian Pines on the Herbert Hoover Dike. The pines were killed but the herbicides inadvertently leached into the soil to the north and killed the stand of lives oaks where the kites subsequently relocated. Communal roosts with large numbers of birds in one place are vulnerable to disturbance either by natural or man made events and just one event can cause the birds to abandon the roost or use valuable fat reserves flying around the roost until they settle back into it.

The FWC conducted a two day experiment in 2006 to determine if the kites could be coaxed to move their roost from the dead oak trees to a more northerly and secluded site where they could roost in live trees. Researchers believe that the dead oaks will eventually start losing their limbs and the kites will have to find a new roost. In addition, the FWC believes a more secure roost site could be accomplished by moving the roost farther away from the Herbert Hoover Dike but not too close to Fisheating Creek where they could be disturbed by boaters, birders, hikers, etc.

Decoys were made to resemble kites and were placed in two oak trees about 200 yards north of the roost. Some of the kites began immediately using the two decoy trees for roosting and returned to the trees the next day as well. Relocation would also require removal of the current roost trees in conjunction with placement of decoys in the new roost trees to encourage kites to use the new roost trees. ARCI believes the results of the test confirm relocation is feasible but fairly risky because removal of the current roost trees may result in the dispersal and fragmentation of the kites to multiple roost sites rather than in the selected decoy trees. ARCI suggested a compromise plan that would establish an alternate roost site using decoys but leaving the current roost trees in place to avoid the risk of removing the current site.

Florida Mottled Duck

Florida has always been an important fall and winter destination for migratory waterfowl with its strategic location at the southern end of the Atlantic Flyway. Almost every species of diving duck and puddle duck can be found here in the winter along with migratory Canada geese and the occasional snow goose, blue goose, or along the coast, the black brant. Traditionally only two species of duck were year round residents in Florida, the wood duck, and the Florida duck also known as the Florida mottled duck. However, in the 1970's the fulvous tree duck of Mexico and coastal Texas became established as a year round resident duck in Florida. And in the early 1980's the black-bellied whistling duck of Mexico and coastal Texas also became established. Both of these relative newcomers are still extending their range within Florida.

The mottled duck is found along the coastal brackish and freshwater marshes of the Gulf Coast from Texas to Alabama. The Florida mottled duck is a unique subspecies of the mottled duck and is found only in peninsular Florida and its population is estimated to be about 30,000 to 40,000 individuals. The Florida mottled duck is found in man-made and natural wetlands associated primarily with the Kissimmee River, Lake Okeechobee and the Everglades Agricultural Area. Researchers believe that the highest densities of Florida mottled ducks are found in Osceola, Okeechobee, Highlands, Glades, Desoto, Charlotte, and Collier Counties. Palm Beach County is also an important breeding area for Florida mottled ducks especially in the Everglades Stormwater Treatment Areas, the marshes of Lake Okeechobee, and the urban ponds and wetlands in the West Palm Beach area.

The Florida mottled duck is also included in the FWC Gaps Report as one of the "Prairie Birds" due to its fondness for wetlands found in association with Florida's unique dry prairie ecosystem. Researchers have found that Florida mottled ducks are cross breeding with domestic mallards which can be found in most urban and suburban storm water ponds, one of the areas the Florida mottled duck has adapted to. The FWC has reported that up to five percent of banded Florida mottled ducks now have mallard plumage characteristics. This cross breeding is creating a hybrid of the Florida mottled duck that threatens to eventually eliminate the pure sub-species of Florida mottled duck.

The FWC Gaps Report indicates that within Glades County, the Florida mottled duck has a high abundance in the vicinity of the State-owned Curry Island near the mouth of Fisheating Creek east of S.R. 78. This area is also shown as a Strategic Habitat Conservation Area (SHCA) for the Florida mottled duck. Not much research has been done on the distribution of the Florida mottled duck but I would speculate that the dry prairie marshes associated with the Fisheating Creek Ecosystem provide habitat as well as the wetlands and improved pastures between Cowbone Marsh and SR 78.

In 1984 the FWC released the findings of research conducted on the status of the Florida mottled duck based on a banding program and subsequent harvest data collected from hunters over a twenty year period between 1961 and 1981. A total of 1,391 ducks were banded over the study period during the months of June through September and of these bands, 205 were recovered. Harvest data was also obtained by FWS surveys and mail questionnaires. In 1978 researchers estimated that up to 19,000 Florida mottled ducks were killed by hunters in Florida which represented approximately eight percent of the total duck harvest for all duck species in the State. Researchers also concluded that hunters killed about 27 percent of the fall population of Florida mottled ducks and that another 36 percent died from non-hunting causes.

Estimates of the total population of Florida mottled ducks for the years between 1977 and 1980 varied between 58,000 and 75,000. Research indicated a significant population decline between the years 1964 and 1980. Researchers suggested that habitat destruction was the largest factor in the decline of the Florida mottled duck noting that channelization and drainage in the Kissimmee River/Lake Okeechobee Basin, the core area for the Florida mottled duck, had resulted in the loss of 52 percent of associated wetlands habitat or almost 870,000 acres. The study concluded that a more reliable method was needed to estimate populations of the Florida mottled duck in order to better mange the species.

The scarcity of information on the natural history of the Florida mottled duck prompted the FWC to initiate a three year study which began in 2008 and is titled "Florida mottled duck Telemetry Report." The first Annual Report was issued in 2009. The report stated that little information is available on how the Florida mottled duck uses its core habitats associated with Lake Okeechobee, the Kissimmee River Basin and the Everglades Agricultural Area and adjacent urban areas. These areas have experienced significant habitat modification primarily for agricultural activities but also as part of the Comprehensive Everglades Restoration Project. The purpose of the study was to better understand the ecology of the Florida mottled duck in south Florida, to determine how relatively recent wetland changes have affected them, and to investigate habitat use, movements, and survival of female Florida mottled ducks. This information will allow land managers and wildlife biologist to more effectively manage and conserve this unique species.

Forty seven females were caught in the Everglades Agricultural Area where they were tagged and radio transmitters were surgically placed in their abdomens. In the West Palm Beach area 16 females were radio-marked as well. Efforts to tag females in the Kissimmee River Basin area failed due to high water following Hurricane Fay. The tagged birds movements were tracked daily using trucks and fixed wing aircraft. Tracking revealed that the everglades birds used flooded fields, ponds/prairies and the Everglades Stormwater Treatment Areas in the fall and early winter. During the dry season from mid winter through early spring they moved to wetter areas including the marshes of the Everglades and marshes on the south and west side of Lake Okeechobee. During the nesting period, the birds move to dryer areas in the vicinity of the Everglades Agricultural Area or if water levels in Lake Okeechobee were low, they nested there as well. Data from the West Palm Beach area birds revealed that in general they inhabited urban ponds and ditches and only moved short distances primarily associated with water level fluctuations in these habitats.

Little information was obtained about nesting and only 11 nests were located. Of these researchers found that the Everglades birds nested in either sugarcane fields or Everglades sawgrass marsh and the West Palm Beach birds nested in a variety of habitats including scrub, pine/palmetto, grassy road medians, or in landscaped areas within housing developments. The study has been completed and a final report was issued on November 2, 2011 entitled "A Conservation Plan For The Florida mottled duck". FWC states that the plan identifies specific actions to maintain the Florida mottled duck at a population level that that can sustain hunting and viewing opportunities in perpetuity and includes goals and objectives for population density, genetic integrity, habitat management, and public information and education".

Florida Sandhill Crane

The Florida sandhill crane is one of six sub-species of sandhill cranes and the only one which resides year-round in Florida and extreme south Georgia. It is most common in Central Florida where it nests in shallow freshwater herbaceous marshes. It stands almost four feet tall and has a unique rattling call which can be heard for several miles on a quite winter days. The only other species of sandhill crane to regularly inhabit Florida is the Greater sandhill crane which is a winter migrate, usually arriving in Florida in October and November and migrating back north as far as Canada and Alaska in February and March.

The Florida sandhill crane is an opportunistic feeder and will feed on aquatic invertebrates and plants, insects, worms, seeds, grains, and small birds and mammals. It prefers to forage on improved pastures or dry prairies followed by shallow wetlands but will also forage in oak hammocks and on agricultural lands. As far as wetlands, they seem to particularly prefer those dominated by pickerel weed and maiden cane. In 1974 the FWC listed the Florida sandhill crane as a threatened species because it determined that the long term survival of the sub-species is at risk due to a loss of its habitat, its small population estimated to be between 4,000 and 6,000 individuals, and its low reproductive potential.

Research has shown that water depth in the shallow freshwater wetlands that they feed and nest in is a primary controlling factor in seasonal shifts in habitat use. Cranes will typically nest at night in wetlands having a depth of between four and twelve inches. They also prefer to forage in wetlands where the water is hock deep or less. Nesting can begin as early as December but typically starts in January and continues through August.

They will not forage in dense wetlands or where vegetation is higher than about 20 inches which limits their ability to spot potential predators. Research has shown that they have become adapted to suburban areas such as airports, golf courses, horse farms, sod farms where grass is retained along with small herbaceous wetlands. They are vulnerable to flying into power lines as well as fences.

The Fisheating Creek region provides good habitat for the Sandhill crane with its abundant pastures, and mosaic of dry prairies and small herbaceous wetlands. The FWC GAPS report identified a Strategic Habitat Conservation Area for the Florida sandhill crane west of Nicodemus Slough as well as an area located south and west of Palmdale to just north of LaBelle.

In the early 1970's the FWC conducted research on the Florida sandhill crane at Fisheating Creek. In 1972-73, eleven Florida sandhill cranes were captured on Cloverdale Farm in Manatee County and released onto the Lykes Fisheating Creek Refuge east of Palmdale where studies were already underway on Florida sandhill cranes. The purpose of the translocation of cranes was to determine dispersal behavior of the cranes in anticipation of future restocking efforts Statewide. Dispersal behavior is an important factor in restocking success of wild trapped animals and determines the minimum number of animals required for restocking. The cranes were captured by using corn containing alpha-chloralose as bait. The narcotized cranes were netted and transported to the release sites. Prior to release they were leg banded and color streamers were also attached for identification purposes. Some were also fitted with colored leg bands. Three of the cranes were observed in the release area up to 10 days after release and two were seen 10 miles west of the release area the following day.

Few cranes were observed at Fisheating Creek after release. Researchers believe this may be because fewer searches were made and also the released cranes may have been driven away by cranes already nesting in the release area. Another possibility given by researchers was that the considerable amount of good quality crane habitat at Fisheating Creek allowed the cranes to disperse without being detected. The study concluded that translocated Florida sandhill cranes will generally stay within the areas where they are relocated as long as the habitat is of good quality and the transfer site is at least 100 miles from the capture site, reducing the likelihood of them returning to where they were captured.

In 1973, the FWC published the results of another study entitled "Capturing Sandhill Cranes Using Alpha-Chloralose." While capturing wild turkeys in Glades and Hardee Counties using the narcotic alpha-chloralose, cranes were attracted to the baited areas resulting in deaths from overdoses. The FWC decided to experiment with different dosages to determine the optimum dosage needed to safely capture the cranes to prevent them from interfering with the turkey trapping efforts. In addition, the data could be used to help in future translocation of cranes using alpha-chloralose for restocking efforts. A total of 266 cranes were captured using alpha-chloralose and 41 were captured using rocket nets for comparison. Much of the trapping took place on the Lykes Fisheating Creek Refuge east of Palmdale. A total of 17 field test were conducted using alpha-chloralose in different dosages.

Unfortunately when the higher dosages were used (up to 2 grams per cup of corn) mortality was as high as 50% due to overdosing or drowning when cranes waded into adjacent wetlands or water bodies. In total, 17% of the 227 cranes captured with alpha-chloralose died. Use of the cannon net resulted in 41 captured cranes of which one was decapitated, two died from broken necks and one died from chocking on corn. The study concluded that the optimum dosage of alpha-chloralose for safely capturing cranes was between .45 and .50 grams per cup of corn and that further research was needed to determine the safest way to capture sandhill cranes whether through drugs, cannon nets, ground traps, etc.

Wood Stork

The Fisheating Creek Ecosystem is a known feeding area for the endangered wood stork and FNAI occurrence records show several locations where the wood stork has been documented. The United States population of wood storks has been in decline since the 1930's due to a decline in the quality and area of its breeding and foraging habitats. In 1984 the FWS designated the wood stork as endangered.

The wood stork has a unique feeding method known as tactolocation or grope feeding that gives it specialized habitat requirements and these habitats have been disrupted by changes in the distribution, timing and quality of water flows, especially in South Florida where they have historically migrated in the winter months. The FWS has reported that in some years the Everglades supports over half the winter wood stork population in the U.S.

The wood stork's northern breeding range is the southern U.S. where it breeds in colonies in Florida, as well as a handful of coastal Counties in Georgia and South Carolina. Outside the U.S. the breeding population of wood storks ranges from northern Argentina through Central America, Mexico, the American Southwest, as well as Cuba and Hispaniola. Historically, prior to its habitat decline, breeding populations of wood storks in the U.S. ranged from Texas to South Carolina. Post breeding populations of wood storks from Florida, Georgia and South Carolina disperse as far north as North Carolina and as far west as Mississippi and Alabama. Post breeding populations of wood storks from Mexico disperse throughout the western U.S and occasionally into Canada.

In Florida, the breeding population of wood storks occurs within colonies located in Broward, Charlotte, Collier, Dade, Hardee, Indian River, Lee, Monroe, Osceola, Palm Beach, Polk, St. Lucie, Sarasota and occasionally Martin County. Winter water levels in the Everglades are a critical factor in the number of feeding wood storks and previous counts have ranged from a low of 1,233 birds during high water to 7,874 birds during low water.

Within South Florida, the National Audubon's Corkscrew Swamp Sanctuary has consistently supported a significant number of nesting wood storks and in fact has the largest wood stork nesting colony in the U.S. Since 1956 Audubon has kept records of nesting wood storks at Corkscrew Swamp Sanctuary. In the late 50's and early 60's Corkscrew accounted for 51% of the total wood stork nests in Florida but the average is 12% of the total Florida nests. The highest count was recorded during the 1960-1961 nesting season when 6,000 pairs of nesting wood storks produced an astounding 17,000 fledglings. The number of nesting wood storks and fledglings has since declined at Corkscrew most probably due to the extensive development related drainage that took place in Southwest Florida in the 60's and 70's. A 1995 survey of Florida wood stork populations identified 5,523 pairs of nesting wood storks of which Corkscrew had 864 pairs or 15% of the state total but which was 87% of the total 996 pairs of nesting wood storks identified in the Everglades/Big Cypress region.

Wood storks generally nest, roost, and forage in freshwater and estuarine wetland habitats. Normally their nests are constructed in trees located within swamps or on islands surrounded by water for added protection against predators. The large nesting colonies in Everglades National Park typically build their nests in cypress or mangrove trees in the estuarine areas at the south end of the Park. During the non-breeding season wood storks forage in a variety of habitats including freshwater marsh, agricultural ponds, roadside and agricultural ditches, tidal creeks and pools, cypress ponds and freshwater sloughs.

The wood storks unique feeding method called tactolocation or grope feeding requires it to feed in shallow water preferably where prey fish are concentrated. With this feeding method the wood stork wades slowly through the water with its partially open beak immersed in the water. When it feels a prey animal, it snaps its beak shut, raises its head and swallows its prey. They will often use their feet to stir the water as they wade which helps to flush hiding prey. Using this method allows them to hunt at night and in water that is cloudy or densely vegetated. However, the down side of this method is that prey needs to be fairly concentrated in low spots such as alligator holes, sloughs, or ponds, for it to be effective. Concentrated prey occurs where water levels are low and ideally where water levels are allowed to fluctuate from high to low without interference from artificial drainage systems.

The loss of wetlands and the alteration of wetlands natural hydrologic cycles in Central and South Florida is the primary threat to the wood stork in the U.S. Historically wood storks began forming nesting colonies in South Florida between November and January, however, since the 1970's habitat alteration has caused them to begin nesting later between February and March. This has resulted in an increase in nests failures and colony abandonment due to a lack of prey for the young: if summer rains begin on time in May and June, the wood stork's prey is dispersed into the flooded marshes and the young nestlings starve to death. Researchers have estimated that it takes an incredible 443 pounds of fish to feed a wood stork family (two adults and two nestlings) during a breeding season, thus the need for a concentrated supply of prey fish.

Fortunately wood storks are still able to feed in coastal creeks and marshes found in South Carolina, Georgia, and Northeast Florida where tidal action concentrates prey during low tide. This may be one of the factors in explaining why the majority of breeding now occurs outside of South Florida, a trend which started in the 1960's with a decrease in nests in South Florida and an increase in nests in North Florida, Georgia and South Carolina. In the two traditional nesting sites found in the Everglades and Big Cypress Swamp, nesting pairs of wood storks declined from 8,500 pairs in 1961 to less than 500 pairs annually between the years 1987 to 1995. On average, South Florida's breeding population of wood storks represents 53% of the Florida breeding population and 34% of the Southeastern breeding population. However, the Everglades and other parts of South Florida are still important winter foraging areas for wood storks.

During the non-breeding season in Florida which corresponds to the rainy season from May through October, young wood storks from South Florida have been tracked throughout the entire wood stork range in the Southeast from Mississippi to South Carolina. Likewise, young from a colony in Georgia have been tracked south the Everglades National Park in the winter. Researchers have concluded that this movement suggests the southeastern population of wood storks is a single population that responds to habitat changes through relocation throughout their range.

The FWS Recovery Plan for the wood stork contains a list of recovery criteria with emphasis on habitat restoration within the traditional nesting areas located within the Everglades as well as the Kissimmee River and Lake Okeechobee Basins. While not known as an important nesting area for wood storks, Fisheating Creek does provide foraging areas important to wood storks. During the 1973-74 nesting season, wood storks at Corkscrew Swamp Sanctuary were monitored by the University of Florida, Center for Wetlands to determine where their feeding areas were located. Surveys were conducted between December 1973 and May 1974 in parts of Collier, Hendry, Lee, Charlotte, and Glades Counties.

Using a single engine aircraft, researchers followed flights of wood storks as they left their roosts in the morning in route to feeding areas. The first week of the monitoring, flights were conducted daily at an average elevation of 300 to 450 feet and thereafter flights were conducted once or twice every two weeks. Researchers identified 38 feeding sites used by wood storks. As sites dried up and became depleted of prey, the wood storks would move to the next site where prey was abundant. In general, the storks moved north to south and initially they fed in wet prairie ponds but switched to wetland slough ponds later in the season since these tended to dry out last.

Of the 38 feeding sites, five were identified in the vicinity of Fisheating Creek where the wood storks fed initially and which was almost 60 miles from the roost, the farthest extent of their feeding. One hundred and twenty five wood storks were observed at these five sites between December 15 and December 21. Interestingly researchers noted that to reach these outlying sites, the wood storks would first ride thermals near Corkscrew Swamp Sanctuary in a circular rising pattern until they reached an altitude of up to 5,000 feet. Once altitude was reached, they would soar toward the feeding site until they again needed to gain altitude. This thermal/soaring pattern was repeated until the site was reached.

The five feeding areas associated with Fisheating Creek were located at Rainey Slough, Chaparral Slough, Fisheating Creek, Nicodemus Slough and Cowbone Marsh. Researchers determined that these five feeding areas along with other areas used at the beginning of the nesting season were used by the adult wood storks as a way to build up energy reserves just prior to egg laying. The other sites were then used later in the season to feed the adults as well as the young.

Researchers concluded that all 38 identified feeding areas were significant feeding sites necessary to sustaining the long term productivity of the Corkscrew Swamp wood storks. Researchers recommended that steps should be taken to preserve all of the sites since the loss of any one of them could impact the wood storks at Corkscrew Sanctuary. Researchers also noted that all of the feeding sites were used concurrently by a high number of other wading birds as well.

Short-Tailed Hawk

The Short-tailed hawk is one of Florida's rarest birds and research on them is limited. This bird of prey is found through much of Mexico and South America but Florida is the only place where it can be found in the United States. Surprisingly, the bird is not listed as threatened or endangered by the FWS most likely due to lack of data to confirm a declining population. It typically breeds in Central Florida and winters in the extreme southern part of the peninsula south of Lake Okeechobee especially in Everglades National Park (ENP) where they inhabit the transition zone between the coastal mangroves and the freshwater marshes and coastal prairies of the Everglades. Occurrence data from FNAI shows at least six occurrence records located throughout the Fisheating Creek project area and the FWC has identified a Strategic Habitat Conservation Area for the hawk at the confluence of Fisheating Creek and Rainey Slough.

After years of speculation, researchers have confirmed that short-tailed hawks do indeed migrate from within Florida from north to south during the winter season beginning in October and then back north in the spring beginning in February to breed in Central Florida. A few also breed in northern Florida. They are specialist in their feeding habits, feeding mostly on small birds, in particular the red-winged blackbird and the meadowlark, but they will also feed occasionally on rodents, snakes and lizards. Researchers have identified six general breeding areas: (a) the Big Bend region of northwest Florida; (b) the Green Swamp in Central Florida; (c) east of Lake Wales; (d) the Okeechobee Plain (Glades, Okeechobee, Highlands Counties); (e) Telegraph Swamp (Babcock Ranch); and (f) the

Big Cypress National Preserve/Everglades National Park.

The short-tailed hawk spends most of its day soaring thermals while hunting for prey. Most often, prey are caught either on the ground, on perches, or in the air in that order, by a sharp nearly vertical stooping dive with wing tips folded against the tail or less often by a shallow angled stooping dive with wings bowed. Occasionally the hawk will search for prey by "kiting" where wings are held open into the wind as the bird remains stationary for a few seconds as he scans below. Kiting is a distinctive behavior helpful in identifying them, along with their distinctive upswept wings in flight similar to the wing position of the vulture.

Because they tend to inhabit dense wetland forests in remote places, their numbers have been hard to quantify. Researchers today believe that there are less than 500 and of these there are an estimated 400 breeding pairs. Researchers have determined that they have low productivity and are thinly distributed. The FWC ranked them first for vertebrates in the need for further research and population surveys.

Between 1966 and 1972, Ornithologist John Ogden studied short-tailed hawks in Florida including Fisheating Creek, ENP and the Florida Keys and he published a paper in the January 1974 issue of "The Auk," the publication of the American Ornithological Society. He identified and studied two active nests at Fisheating Creek, one at Hutto Cow Camp east of Palmdale and the other at Rock Lake on Fisheating Creek just east of Palmdale as well. He collected regurgitated food pellets and undigested food at the Hutto Cow Camp nest in 1968 and between 1970 and 1972 at the Rock Lake nest site where there was a white phase of the short -tailed hawk (the hawk has a white and a dark phase). He also spent hours at these two nests observing the hawks hunting techniques and food preferences. At Rock Lake he noted that doves seemed to make up two thirds of the prey base. Ogden was also the first to suggests that the hawks migrated within Florida and radio telemetry data has since confirmed this. Researchers noted that radio-tagged birds migrating south to wintering grounds in ENP and the Keys preferred to pass west of Lake Okeechobee rather than flying over the Lake.

Ogden wrote: "The Fisheating Creek region of Glades County supports the greatest density of nesting Short-tails presently known, where three or four pairs are resident within 5 miles of the Town of Palmdale. Fisheating Creek and its tributaries there are narrowly bordered by strands and isolated patches of cypress, long-needled pines, swamp hardwoods, and several species of evergreen oaks. These woodlands finger through expansive prairies and pastures dominated by saw palmetto (Serona Repens), native grasses and herbs. Two pairs of Short-tailed hawks studied here built their nests in tall pine or cypress trees less than 75 m inside a stand of woods, and did most of their hunting over the prairie and brushland adjacent to their nesting sites." Ogden noted that Fisheating Creek was used by short-tailed hawks year round as both breeding and wintering areas. Records kept by others between 1881 and 1971 support this and note winter sightings of Short-tail hawks on the north and west sides of Lake Okeechobee.

The Avian Research and Conservation Institute in Gainesville conducted studies for the FWC on the short-tailed hawk and published a Final Report in 2005. This study provided valuable information on the natural history of the hawks and provided conclusions and recommendations for conserving this species. The goal of the study was to identify nests in the breeding areas, monitor the nests to determine nest success and productivity rates, determine breeding season range sizes and foraging habitats of adults, determine survival rates and causes of death for tagged young, and to determine range size and foraging habitats of tagged winter adults and young.

Researchers caught and radio-tagged 20 short-tailed hawks in their winter habitats at ENP and the Florida Keys. The birds were lured into range with live birds and once caught were fitted with tiny radio transmitters. The hawks were then tracked to their summer breeding areas and nest were found using fixed wing aircraft. Once the nests were found, researchers also tagged the young just before they fledged. In all, 38 hawks were radio tagged and one was fitted with a satellite receiver. The nests and young were monitored for four years. Twenty seven nests were located within 14 nesting territories of ten counties in Central Florida. Seven of the 14 territories were on private lands and seven were on protected private or public conservation lands. Nests were usually located in dense wetland forest near or adjacent to lakes or streams. Preferred nesting trees in order of preference were loblolly pine, red bay, bald cypress and red maple. In addition, one nest was located in a black mangrove tree.

Several conclusions were made from this study. The population of Short-tail hawks is small, less than 500, which makes them susceptible to catastrophic weather (i.e hurricanes), disease, loss of suitable habitat, human persecution and genetic anomalies. In addition, the hawks are vulnerable due to low reproductivity and low nesting success. One positive finding was that survival rates for first year young were good. Nests were mostly found in large stands of wetland forests on private lands which are vulnerable to harvest. However, the study concluded that loss of foraging habitat was the single greatest threat to the continued existence of the short-tailed hawk. The study also conclude that based on the known distribution of short-tailed hawks in Florida, there are not sufficient populations on protected public lands to maintain the population. The study recommended that a long term monitoring plan be initiated in order to determine if the short-tailed hawk meets the requirement for Federal listing based on declining populations.

Protection of the Fisheating Creek Ecosystem will help to ensure the existence of many species of Prairie birds and hopefully provide opportunities to manage habitats that will increase the populations and health of many of these bird species including the short-tailed hawk.

RECENT DEVELOPMENT PRESSURES

Glades Power Park

In 2006, Florida Power and Light (FPL) began talks with Glades County officials about building a 1,960 megawatt power plant with a 500 foot tall, 30 foot wide emission stack on 4,900 acres of agricultural land owned by Lykes approximately five miles northwest of Moore Haven. On September 6, 2006 FPL announced that it had plans to build the Glades Power Park after Glades County approved the project. FPL picked this site because of its adequate acreage, adequate groundwater supplies, and proximity to multiple rail lines for efficient coal shipments. The project was to be know as the Glades Power Park. FPL intended to use pulverized coal technology rather than the cleaner burning integrated gasification combined cycle process (IGCC). FPL had originally approached the St. Lucie County Commission to build the plant in that County, but in 2005 St. Lucie County rejected the request and FPL headed to Glades County.

Environmental groups opposed the project for numerous reasons including the impacts to the Everglades from mercury emissions and impacts to air quality from carbon dioxide (13 million tons per year) and sulfur emissions; impacts to groundwater in the upper Floridan Aquifer (26 mgd); and the proximity of the project to Fisheating Creek located just five miles to the north. Some opponents of the project thought that the project should be approved only if it used the cleaner burning IGCC process but most felt that no new coal fired plants should be built so close to the Everglades which has already been affected by mercury pollution from existing coal fired plants in South Florida. FPL stated that the facility would generate an average 21 million per year in property taxes and create 180 full time positions.

The northern property line of the FPL site abutted the southern boundary of Nicodemus Slough which is a tributary to Lake Okeechobee and part of the Fisheating Creek Ecosystem Florida Forever project. Opponents of the power plant accused Glades County of quietly changing the County Zoning Ordinance to allow the Glades Power Park on the Lykes agriculturally zoned site just prior to the Florida Public Service Commission (PSC) hearings. Prior to this change, power plants were not one of the allowed uses on lands zoned Agriculture. Glades County officials denied this and stated that the zoning code was changed to allow FPL to provide power to the recently approved Muse Village DRI north of LaBelle on adjacent land zoned Agriculture.

Fortunately, in 2007, the PSC denied the FPL petition for a Determination of Need to build the power plant. The PSC based their denial on the fact that FPL could not show the coal plant was not the most cost effective alternative and that there was too much uncertainty regarding future fuel costs and the carbon regulatory market. No doubt the current awareness of the effects coal fired power plants have on global warming contributed to the PSC decision. Shortly after the PSC denial, Governor Crist announced support of the PSC decision.

The Heartland Parkway

On July 1, 2006. Florida Trend Magazine published an in depth article about a Central Florida toll road to be known as the Heartland Parkway which was being promoted by politicians, large landowners and the business community. Florida's Heartland consists of seven Counties: Polk, Highlands, Hardee, Okeechobee, Desoto, Glades and Hendry.

According to Florida Trend, Orlando attorney J. Charles Gray, representing rural landowners, sketched a map of this road which would run 100 miles north to south from I-4 in Polk County south to Lee County east of Ft. Myers. The proposed route straddled the county lines separating Desoto and Highlands Counties as well as Charlotte and Glades Counties just west of Fisheating Creek and if approved would undoubtedly open up all these rural Counties to even more growth pressures. In Glades and Highlands Counties the proposed route includes land owned by Lykes who, along with other large landowners on the route, have gone on record as being in support of this proposed toll road. Gray sent the map to the Florida Turnpike Enterprise (FTE), a division of the Florida Department of Transportation (FDOT).

Others assisting in this effort included former lawmaker Rick Danzler and former Florida Senator and Central Florida citrus grower and rancher, J.D. Alexander. Alexander is the grandson of the late Ben Hill Griffin who owned large tracts of land in Central Florida including the Blue Head Ranch. As currently proposed, the toll road will traverse through the Blue Head Ranch development. Alexander is the current CEO of Alico the major stockholder of Atlantic Blue Corporation, owner of Blue Head Ranch.

In March 2006, the FTE formally announced the proposed Heartland Parkway along with another road proposed by the same group known as the Heartland Coast To Coast which would run east west through Central Florida. The Heartland Coast to Coast was also influenced by Manatee County Commissioner Joe McClash and by the Sebring Airport Authority which made the road part of its Master Plan. These roads were proposed by a small group of power brokers who determined both routes before the Florida Turnpike Authority had even conducted a feasibility study of the routes including potential environmental impacts and without any public input.

Not surprisingly, after the FTE announced their consideration of the proposed toll roads, State and environmental officials along with local government officials expressed their concern and many had not heard about it until it had been announced in local newspapers. Highlands County officials have been trying for decades to get a major highway built through their county. Highlands, Polk, Desoto, Glades, Okeechobee, Hardee and Hendry counties have been designated as "Rural Areas of Critical Economic Concern" partly due to a lack of infrastructure to support and attract businesses and people.

The Florida Trend article referenced Lakeland Realtor Dean Sanders who brokers large agricultural tracts for farmers throughout the heartland. Sanders stated that some longtime ranchers are moving to North Florida, Georgia, or Alabama where land is cheaper and taxes are lower and who question why they should continue to ranch on land that cost $20,000 an acre. Heartland landowners, including ranchers and citrus growers, have stated they would donate considerable acreage along the highway corridor as well as conservation easements in exchange for increased residential densities and development rights elsewhere, a sort of de-facto transfer of development rights.

Critics of the proposed toll road have stated that it would be a stimulus to growth instead of a response to growth and the Florida Turnpike Authority has been criticized in the past for proposing roads that would trigger rampant growth, which they deny. The State Bureau of Economic and Business Research has projected a population increase of 70,000 in the six Heartland Counties designated as Rural Areas of Critical Economic Concern between 2000 and 2020 without the road, but with the road, his population projection estimate increased to an astounding 700,000. According to FTE, the State does not have the funding to fix and expand existing roads, let alone build new roads such as the Heartland Parkway. If this road is eventually built, it will most likely be funded jointly by both public and private resources with right of way being donated by land owners and interchanges and exits being built and paid for by developers.

An article in the February 2, 2007 Tampa Tribune states that the FDOT sees the Heartland Parkway as a way to provide relief to other north south roads in the region including I-75, U.S. 17 and U.S. 27. FDOT has also stated that the road would function as another route for hurricane evacuation and has included it on FDOT's "New Corridors Study Map". A group of landowners pushing for the new toll road has formed and is known as HEART (Heartland Economic and Agricultural Rural Task Force). HEART has stated that the toll road will do more than just convert agricultural lands into other uses, it will also be an economic and quality of life corridor with accompanying utility, rail, telecommunications, and wildlife corridors built into it along the route along with strict growth rules. HEART states that the toll road route is owned by a relatively few land owners who are also willing to cooperate, making it possible to Master Plan on a multi-county regional scale. The Florida Wildlife Federation has stated they are willing to listen to HEART's proposals before making a decision whether to support the toll road.

The Heartland Parkway is one of nine north/south corridors in the Florida Transportation Commissions study which aims to ease congestion from projected growth in the next 20 to 30 years. If built, it will likely start in Polk County and be built to the south as funds become available. Current estimates of the cost are approximately $3.5 billion. Supporters say that it must be planned now because if we wait too long, development may close off the opportunity to build the road within the proposed corridor. The State must perform preliminary design and engineering studies to determine the feasibility and costs.

Currently U.S. 27 is one of the few viable north/south truck freight routes and it's already over capacity. HEART has been meeting with environmental and planning organizations and Rick Danzler has stated that "we want this to be the most environmentally conscious route in the history of the U.S." Dantzler and HEART point out that features of the toll road will include enormous undeveloped space surrounding the corridor; extensive wildlife corridors including fencing to protect bears and panthers; clustering and open space; limited access; wetland preservation and; rail and utility corridors. Hardee, Glades and Desoto County Commissions have endorsed the toll road as have the City Commissions of Winter Haven and Haines City.

However, in 2007 Governor Crist went on record in opposition to the toll road and called it the "Road To Nowhere." Crist stated that expanding already overburdened urban roads is of greater priority than building new rural highways. The FTA has stated that both the north/south and the east/west toll roads are feasible and will cost $7.824 billion of which only $1.153 billion could be raised through selling bonds. So for awhile it appeared the north south toll road was on the back burner.

Fast forward to 2012 with Governor Rick Scott at the helm. The following is from the Tampa Bay Times article on March 1, 2012: "Despite a $1.4 billion budget shortfall and at times heated rhetoric about finding ways to spend fewer state dollars, budget writers have tucked $34.7 million into this year's proposed spending plan for the design of a portion of the Heartland Parkway, a long-dormant road project in Central Florida. Rick Scott's decision to embrace this expensive boondoggle has also exposed his continued preference for cronyism over merit in determining whom he involves in major decisions. If lawmakers approve the state's proposed transportation work plan, which includes billions of dollars for hundreds of other projects, about $18 million could be spent on the Polk project starting this summer. Another $16.7 million is earmarked for 2014 or 2015."

Eagle Security Training Center

During a Highlands County Commission meeting in 2008, the Highlands County Commission was asked by Lake County businessman Seth Ellis to expedite permitting for a war games facility to be referred to as the Eagle Security Training Center, a live fire training center for the military, Homeland Security, local police forces, and even foreign governments. The facility was to be located on 12 square miles of land in the southwest corner of the county where Highlands County meets Glades, Desoto and Charlotte counties. The land, known as Southern Farms, was owned by Lakeland businessman Ron Grigsby and was formerly used to grow citrus. At the meeting, Ellis was introduced to the Commission by Bert Harris Jr., a well known property rights attorney who is know for the Bert Harris Act. This act requires local governments to provide relief or compensation to a private property owner when it can be shown that a government land use regulation has "inordinately burdened" existing use of a real property.

Mr. Ellis described the concept of the project to the Commissioners stating that it could include up to 100,000 square feet of classrooms and administrative facilities, 40,000 square feet of military style shoot houses, three five story training buildings, 1,000 dorm rooms, 25 single family homes, 100 multi-family apartments, two 250 foot training towers, and last but not least, a 6,000 foot long runway. The interior 2,000 acres would be designed as a live fire training area with use of weapons shooting ammunition up to 50 caliber in size. The project was touted as a job creator with up to 250 jobs and 1,000 students.

The site for the proposed facility was to be located just a few miles west of the rural unincorporated community of Venus in northern Glades County. Venus residents, as well as other residents in southern Highlands and northern Glades County, realized that this massive project, if approved, would dramatically change their way of life as well as threaten the wildlife and water quality of Fisheating Creek. They began to mobilize in opposition to the project. Some residents feared the facility would be used to train mercenaries similar to the large Blackwater Operation in North Carolina or as a live fire training facility for the military. Eagle denied that mercenaries would be trained at the facility. There was also concern that the facility would have round the clock live fire which could be dangerous as well as loud, and that large military style aircraft would be landing and taking off from the new runway at all hours.

All of the public hearings with the Highlands County Planning and Zoning Commission (PZC) and County Commission were filled with those in opposition to the project. However, the proponents of the Training Center were not very forthcoming on details of the facility at the public hearings. In any case, in 2009 the Highlands County PZA voted to approve a rezoning on the parcel from Agriculture to Agriculture with a Planned Development District and forwarded this recommendation to the BCC for their consideration. In 2009 the Highlands County BCC voted to create a new Future Land Use category known as "Agriculture - Training Center" to accommodate the proposed project and they also approved a change to the Future Land Use Map designation on the site from "Agriculture" to "Agriculture - Training Center" and transmitted these Comprehensive Plan amendments to the Department of Community Affairs.

The DCA issued a Notice of Intent to find the Proposed Comprehensive Plan Amendments "Not In Compliance". DCA based their noncompliance finding on the fact that "the Departments primary concerns relate to water supply and protection of the natural resources associated with Fisheating Creek, including wetlands, floodplains and water quality. DCA also recommended that the County and the developer of the Eagle Training Center "work closely with department staff and South Florida Water Management District to identify appropriate remedial actions and amendments."

According to comments submitted to DCA from the South Florida Water Management District (SFWMD), approximately 50% of the site is within the Fisheating Creek sub-basin drainage area and is drained by John Henry Slough and Gannett Slough which both discharge into Fisheating Creek. The remainder of the site is within the Peace River drainage basin managed by the Southwest Florida Water Management District. SFWMD stated that Fisheating Creek is one of three watersheds within the Lake Okeechobee drainage basin which contribute disproportionately high levels of phosphorus into Lake Okeechobee and which must be reduced by 2015 to meet the standards in the Department of Environmental Protection's (DEP) Total Maximum Daily Load water quality program.

In addition, DEP stated that Fisheating Creek is impaired from low dissolved oxygen, high iron levels as well as excessive nutrients. DEP was concerned that an increase in impervious surface levels associated with the training center would result in storm water runoff into the wetlands, Fisheating Creek and ultimately into Lake Okeechobee and DEP said adequate data addressing this issue was not provided in the transmittal document to DCA. DEP also stated that the facility would require groundwater but that inadequate data was supplied to address this issue including the source of the groundwater and the quantity required.

Knowing that water quality and quantity were prime reason for DCA's concerns and ultimately to DCA's finding the amendment package Not In Compliance, the Director of Highlands County Development Services, incomprehensibly suggested to the County Commission that the County negotiate an agreement with DCA that DCA not use the water quality criteria contained in Objective 12 of the Highlands County Comprehensive Plan in their review of the County Comprehensive Plan Amendments for Eagle Training Center. The chairman of the County Commission, wisely stated that Objective 12 of the Comprehensive Plan was "not negotiable."

Eventually, after a lengthy public hearing with a standing room only crowd in opposition to the Eagle Training Center, the Highlands County Board of County Commissioners unanimously turned down the project including the rezoning request, the proposed Future Land Use amendment and the proposed settlement document. However, even though the proposed Future Land Use Amendment to the parcel was denied, the previously approved new Future Land Use category of Agriculture - Training Center remains in the Comprehensive Plan which means that Eagle or any other similar training facility could request a land use and zoning change for a similar project in the future. To prevent this, opponents are seeking to have the new Future Land Use designation rescinded.

It turns out that before coming to Highlands County to seek approval for the Eagle Training Center, the project had gone before the Marion County Commission in Ocala to seek approval for the facility in that county, but it was denied as well.

Bluehead Ranch

Recent attention to the upper Fisheating Creek area has been generated by a mixed use development proposed on the Blue Head Ranch located in the heart of the Fisheating Creek headwaters. The Florida Department of Community Affairs reviewed a request by Atlantic Blue Corporation for an amendment to the Highlands County Comprehensive Plan which includes creation of a new Future Land Use category to be known as the Blue Head Ranch Sustainable Community Overlay District. This overlay is located on 50,000 of the 65,000 acres owned by Atlantic Blue Corporation known as Blue Head Ranch in southwest Highlands County within the headwaters of Fisheating Creek. Atlantic Blue Corporation was headed up by former State Senator J.D. Alexander who is now the current CEO of Alico the major stockholder of Atlantic Blue Corporation.

Currently the ranch is a working cattle ranch which also grows citrus, sod, blueberries and strawberries. Blue Head Ranch is massive and contains over a hundred square miles of land consisting of improved pasture, sod fields, citrus groves, blueberry and strawberry fields as well as numerous wetlands associated with the headwaters of Fisheating Creek. The ranch's southern boundary is located approximately four miles north of the Glades County line and runs north for over 15 miles with S.R. 70 crossing through the middle of the ranch from east to west.

As originally proposed, the overlay district would allow construction of a mixed use project on 7,500 acres in an area to be designated as a Compact Urban Development Area (CUDA). The CUDA as proposed will be in the center of the overlay and bisected by S.R. 70 with approximately 4,500 acres adjacent to the north side of S.R. 70 and the remaining 3,000 acres adjacent to the south side of S.R. 70. According to the applicant's environmental consultant, "the CUDA has been designed to maximize the use of existing farm fields and disturbed agricultural areas and minimize impacts to wetlands and/or unique uplands." The remaining 42,500 acres of the overlay would be designated as a Sustainable Green Assets Area (SGA) which is a "sending area" because it would send development rights to the 7,500 CUDA. Most of the SGA is proposed to be located south of S.R. 70 and a small portion will be located north of S.R. 70.

On the surface this clustering plan seems to have some merit however, the devil is in the details and more details are needed on how the SGA sending areas will be protected and preserved. Normally sending areas are afforded major protection and typically have a conservation easement placed on them. However, according to the transmittal document, the SGA sending area would retain the current Agriculture land use category which would allow all non-urban uses some of which could be quite intense including asphalt plants, community colleges, wastewater treatment plants and cemeteries.

An Environmental Supplement (ES) to the Sustainable Community Overlay was submitted as part of the 2010 EAR Based Amendments which include the proposed Blue Head Ranch Overlay. Vegetation surveys were completed of the overlay lands as part of the ES and of the 50,167 acres in the overlay, four land cover types cover over 87% of the property: improved pasture (18,462 acres or 36.8%), wetlands (12,487 acres or 24.9%), saw palmetto prairie (12,907 acres or 25.7%) and oak hammock (4,033 acres or 8%). Listed species of animals observed on the property included Florida sandhill crane, Audubon's crested caracara, bald eagle, Florida scrub jay, wood stork, snowy egret, white ibis, little blue heron, tri-colored heron, black bear, Sherman's fox squirrel, and gopher tortoise. In addition, the Florida Fish and Wildlife Conservation Commission stated that a collared Florida panther (FP 130) had been confirmed using the north central part of the property during a four month period from December 2004 through March 2005.

The applicant emphasized the benefits of preserving most of the land south of S.R. 70 within the SGA and stated that "Blue Head Ranch, uniquely located between the Archbold Biological Research Station and SWFWMD Bright Hour Ranch Watershed parcel (conservation easement), provides the opportunity to preserve these habitats and create an east-west ecological linkage." This point is later re-emphasized again in the document with the statement that "clearly the identification of the SWFWMD Bright Hour Ranch conservation area on the west and the Archbold Biological Station lands on the east highlight the need to create an east-west linkage, which the proposed plan amendment for Blue Head Ranch would accomplish."

As originally presented, at buildout, the project could include up to 30,000 dwelling units, 8.5 million square feet of office/retail, 1.5 million s.f. of industrial, 900 hotel rooms, and 1 million square feet of public/quasi-public uses. The ranch had originally proposed applying for the Rural Lands Stewardship program but then withdrew the application.

In June 2010 DCA submitted their Objections, Recommendations and Comments Report for the EAR based Comprehensive Plan amendments transmitted by Highlands County. Regarding the County's proposed Blue Head Ranch Sustainable Community Overlay land use category, DCA had numerous objections and in their cover letter they stated that they objected

111

to the overlay because it is some distance to the county's proposed Urban Growth Area boundary and Highlands County should not subsidize the cost of extending water and sewer services to the site.

In addition, DCA objected to the overlay because the supporting data and analysis did not provide enough detail to show there was adequate groundwater capacity in the Floridan Aquifer to serve this development Regarding wastewater, the project would generate up to 4.5 million gallons per day of treated wastewater effluent from the maximum 27,600 residents and 4.9 million square feet of non-residential uses. The data stated that wastewater to be generated by this development would be treated prior to reuse or disposal and that wastewater reuse would be used to irrigate parks, golf courses, common areas, open space and residential yards. If wastewater effluent were also to be discharged offsite, the data and analysis did not address whether or not it would be discharged into tributaries of Fisheating Creek, which happen to run through the CUDA development area.

Another DCA objection was based on the lack of data and analysis addressing how the development would protect Fisheating Creek from additional nutrient loading resulting from the additional storm water runoff created by the development. DCA reminded the applicant that Fisheating Creek is a verified impaired water body due to excessive nutrients and iron, and low dissolved oxygen and that the creek is also an important tributary to Lake Okeechobee, a regionally significant potable water source for South Florida.

DCA also objected that the specific locations of the CUDA and SGA areas were not identified and the SGA areas would retain their Agriculture land use allowing almost all non-urban uses. DCA suggested that lands in the SGA be further designated as either Agriculture for agricultural lands or Resource Protection for resource lands associated with Fisheating Creek and that these areas be identified on maps. DCA also suggested that the SGA's include requirements for a conservation easement rather than the proposed covenants to guarantee protection of sensitive natural resources. The conservation easement should also allow the County and a non-profit conservation organization to be designated as third party beneficiaries to enforce the terms and conditions of the easements. DCA requested more information on how the wetlands associated with Fisheating Creek would be protected within the CUDA.

DCA stated that the Blue Head Ranch Overlay was not supported with data which showed a need for the large development based on population projections provided in the Comprehensive Plan. In addition, the overlay did not discourage Urban Sprawl because it allowed significant amounts of urban development within rural areas at a substantial distance from existing urban areas while leaping over undeveloped which are available and suitable for development. DCA recommended that the County either not adopt the amendment or alternately provide additional data and analysis to show the overlay was needed to accommodate the projected population identified in the Comprehensive Plan and provide additional data and analysis to demonstrate that the overlay will discourage urban sprawl.

The FWC did not object to the overlay, finding it would have equal or less impact than what was currently allowed which was 10,000 dwelling units based on one unit per five acres in the Agriculture Land Use category. FWC also said that the development in the southwest part of the County may take pressure off development now occurring along the Lake Wales Ridge where there are many rare and endangered species of endemic plants and animals. FWC also stated that by concentrating development within the 15% of the 50,000 acres, the project would reduce potential conflicts between humans and wildlife and help preserve a significant wildlife corridor as well.

In 2011 the Department of Community Affairs (now called the Department of Economic Opportunity) found the Highlands County Comprehensive Plan Amendment creating the Blue Head Ranch Overlay District "In Compliance." The only bright spot for Fisheating Creek which traverses the eastern portion of the project in the headwaters area is that a large majority of the project south of SR 70 will be preserved as conservation and agriculture. Before development can take place the project will still need to apply for rezoning of the project through the public hearing process as well as subsequent approval of construction plans. As I said before, the devil will be in the details.

Not long after approval of the Blue Head Ranch Overlay, that portion of the project located south of SR 70 containing 40,559 acres including almost 10 miles of the upper Fisheating Creek corridor was added to the Florida Forever Land Acquisition list in 2012 with a tax assessed value of $12 million. The project had formerly been on the Florida Forever list prior to the request for an overlay but was removed per a request by the landowners.

Interestingly, only a year and a half after approval of the Comprehensive Plan Amendment for Blue Head Ranch, Atlantic Blue Corporation announced in January 2013 that it would attempt to sell most of the Blue Head Ranch assets in Highlands and Desoto Counties totaling over 65,000 acres which includes the the 50,000 acre Blue Head Ranch Overlay. The reason given was the current business climate and the recent change in tax laws that increased taxes for large landowners.

As Florida continues to grow, development pressures are pushing towards the Fisheating Creek area threatening its water quality, wetlands, habitats of listed species of plants and animals, wildlife corridors, as well as the areas aesthetics and quality of life. These development proposals will need to be carefully scrutinized to make sure they are compatible with maintaining the qualities that make Fisheating Creek such a special and unique place.

THE COWBONE MARSH CANOE TRAIL CONTROVERSY

Another issue   regarding Fisheating Creek has recently developed in Cowbone Marsh located approximately five miles upstream from Ft. Center in the lower section of the creek. This is a very remote marshy section of the creek located between Palmdale on the west and SR 78 on the east. The creek channel disappears just west of Cowbone Marsh and then reforms again just east of the marsh and continues all the way to Lake Okeechobee. Some maps and documents refer to Cowbone Marsh as the entire lower area of Fisheating Creek from the point where the creek channel first disappears eastward to the SR 78 bridge.

Generally however, Cowbone Marsh proper is an oblong shaped marsh which is approximately 3 miles long north to south and about a mile and a half wide east to west.   The marsh is dominated primarily by Carolina Willow but also contains shrubs and herbaceous wetland plants. According to historical documents, prior to disruptions to hydrology and water quality, it consisted of more open herbaceous marsh vegetation. The question of navigability on this section of the creek played a key role in the ten year legal battle over ownership of the creek corridor within Glades County.

From the Canoe Outpost at Palmdale, canoeist can travel downstream on Fisheating Creek for approximately nine miles before the channel disappears and the creek's water begins to sheet flow through a large cypress slough for about 1.5 miles where it then transitions into the more marshy section of Cowbone Marsh before the channel reappears again, flowing for another ten miles through the   floodplain marshes and unimproved pasture before discharging into Lake Okeechobee. Paddlers have supposedly navigated this three and a half mile section of the un-channelized creek corridor during high water using GPS, however only experienced paddlers should try this.

One of the mandates in the Fisheating Creek Settlement Agreement, albeit open to interpretation, calls for the FWC to "maintain and enhance navigation in Fisheating Creek". The Settlement Agreement is incorporated into the Fisheating Creek Wildlife Management Plan and enforcement is overseen by a citizens group set up by the DEP Division of State Lands called the Settlement Agreement Advisory Board (SAAB). The SAAB is made up of representatives from Save Our Creeks, Inc., Audubon of Florida, Lykes, and the Environmental Confederation of Southwest Florida.   The Settlement Agreement requires that the state maintain and enhance the navigability of Fisheating Creek through a navigation maintenance program. The FWC has removed fallen logs and invasive aquatic plants in the navigable portions of the creek but previously did not aggressively manage that portion of the Creek within Cowbone Marsh. FWC met with SFWMD and U.S. Army Corps of Engineers (COE) to let them know that FWC was being asked to undertake the Cowbone Marsh project by the SAAB.

Pursuant to this request, FWC began discussing the feasibility of opening up and maintaining a navigational channel through the cypress slough and the un-channelized western portion of Cowbone Marsh in order to create a continuous canoe trail along Fisheating Creek from Ingram's Crossing all the way downstream to Lake Okeechobee. The channel through the cypress slough and Cowbone Marsh would be just large enough to accommodate canoe, kayaks and maybe small motor boats. Currently, the vegetation and underlying muck in the cypress slough and Cowbone Marsh is so thick that during the dry season these areas function as a de-facto dam which maintains 18 to 20 inches of head (higher water) within Fisheating Creek upstream of Cowbone Marsh. Ideally, the navigation channel would be located along the same route identified on a 1929 map of Fisheating Creek produced by the COE. This map was used in the Lykes lawsuit as evidence by those arguing that Cowbone Marsh had been navigable at one time.

In 2008, a group consisting of the FWC, the SFWMD and the COE met at Fisheating Creek to conduct surveys of the cypress slough and Cowbone Marsh and to discuss the options to open and maintain a navigation channel within these areas. Those surveys by both air and ground as well as reviews of aerial photos did not reveal any evidence of the 1929 channel depicted on the old COE map. Following the survey, the consensus seemed to be that if a navigation channel was created, it would only be navigable during the rainy season when water levels were highest from July through October.

Options for opening a channel were discussed including using a machine called a "cookie cutter" which floats in two or more feet of water and chews up the vegetation with two large propeller type blades located in the front as it moves forward to create a channel of between 10 to 25 feet in width. The use of the cookie cutter could be problematic because the upper 1.5 miles of Cowbone Marsh contains large stands of dense willow trees several inches in diameter as well as cypress trees, both of which would be hard to cut through. Another machine discussed was a "marshmaster" which is a large aquatic mowing machine on amphibious pontoons. This machine too could have problems cutting through thick stands of willow and cypress trees.

It was determined that a navigation channel would need to be at least 25 feet wide to allow two motor boats to safely pass. The downside to this is that is would allow large power boats or airboats to come up Fisheating Creek from Lake Okeechobee which could conflict with smaller canoes and kayaks and be a safety issue and also cause stream side erosion from boat wakes. Larger and faster motor boats or airboats could also disrupt wading birds which are common in Cowbone Marsh year round as well as the swallowtail kites which congregate in a large roost located just south of Cowbone Marsh proper in the summer prior to their fall migration south. The group discussed limiting the size of outboard boat motors or only allowing electric motors as a possible options.

SFWMD and COE identified several environmental concerns with opening up a navigation route through Cowbone Marsh which could include tree removal and dredging; impacts to the hydrology of the creek, especially concerns that restoring flow through Cowbone Marsh may lower upstream water levels; and lastly, potential water quality impacts a channel could have by allowing nutrients now filtered by the marsh to flow directly into Lake Okeechobee thereby adding additional phosphorous to the lake. The FWC recommended that a proposed route through the marsh be sprayed with herbicides aerially, followed a couple of months later by a survey of the route's water levels and bottom conditions. After the survey, the group could discuss the feasibility of identified options once again.

In 2009, herbicides were applied aerially to a path through Cowbone Marsh which corresponded roughly to the area indicated on the 1929 COE map as the navigable channel through the marsh. The total area sprayed covered about 20 acres. After the sprayed vegetation had time to die and during high water conditions, the FWC scouted both ends of the 1929 route. From Ft. Center they traveled by airboat up the creek until the channel ended and were then able to go for about another mile before having to stop. From the west they traveled by swamp buggy to the start of the 1929 channel where they then tried to go downstream using kayaks starting at the 1929 channel but due to thick aquatic vegetation were only able to go about 200 yards.

In 2010, another scouting trip was attempted on foot during low water conditions. Starting on the west at the beginning of the 1929 route they were able to go just over a third of a mile but had to turn around due to high water levels and thick vegetation. In all, only 0.75 miles of the 1929 route remained un-surveyed.

After the scouting was completed, a FWC contractor began working on the navigation channel in Cowbone Marsh working upstream (west) with a cookie-cutter machine along the route where the aerial herbicide spraying had occurred. The work was supposed to involve the removal of floating vegetation and the cutting of small brush and trees (without dredging, which would have required State permits). Unfortunately, the work not only involved cutting vegetation but also involved cutting the underlying muck and mineralized soil below that. As the work progressed through the marsh, the dredged and cut materials were shredded and deposited on both sides of the cut.

Water levels in the cut began to decline due to drought conditions so a sandbag dam was placed in the downstream end of the cut to raise water levels. This was done to keep the cookie-cutter floating as it worked its way upstream. However, the work was soon halted due to the inability of the shredding vessel to continue working in the low water conditions. When work stopped, only a third of a mile was left to complete the trail through Cowbone Marsh. The completed portion of the cut was approximately 10 to 12 feet wide.

However, this work had unforeseen consequences when water levels in the creek began to rise from rainfall. The contractor began to see significant amounts of both groundwater and surface water flowing downstream through the cut due to rising water levels upstream of Cowbone Marsh. The increased flow resulted in scouring and erosion of the cut as well as deposition of silt and sand into Fisheating Creek and Cowbone Marsh which began working its way downstream towards Lake Okeechobee.

When DEP was notified of this situation, they quickly determined that it was an immediate threat to the health, safety and welfare to the public and subsequently issued an Emergency Final Order to the FWC. DEP found that the upcoming rainy season would increase flows downstream through the cut causing increased sedimentation downstream and possibly lowering water levels upstream or worst case scenario, even draining the Fisheating Creek watershed upstream. The order required FWC to stop the work and to place temporary sandbags in the cut to reduce flows. The order also required FWC to develop a plan to maintain water levels in the cut so they would be consistent with the pre-cut groundwater levels in Cowbone Marsh. The order also required FWC to apply to DEP for an Environmental Resource Permit (ERP) to authorize activities identified in the FWC plan within 90 days of the order and that all work authorized by the ERP should be initiated within 180 days of issuance of the ERP and completed no later than two years after issuance.

Shortly after the DEP Emergency Order was issued, the COE also became aware of the situation and provided the FWC with a Cease and Desist Order stating that pursuant to the Federal Clean Water Act the FWC was conducting dredge and fill activities in Waters of the United States without a permit. FWC was ordered to "provide information concerning the public and/or private need for this work, the beneficial and detrimental effects it will have on the surrounding environment, and any information you may wish to provide concerning the history of your activity." The COE also stated in their Order that they would provide a copy of the notification to the EPA for their review and coordination.

The COE and EPA stated that the work was not consistent with the Fisheating Creek Settlement Agreement which specifically does not allow dredging Pursuant to Section 25(b): "The navigability of Fisheating Creek throughout the entire Expanded Corridor shall be maintained and enhanced through a navigation maintenance program which includes aquatic weed control and removal of fallen logs and similar obstructions. This section does not authorize dredging."

In 2010, FWC sent DEP a letter requesting permission to place a temporary riser weir about half of the way into the existing cut to address and comply with the issues raised in the Emergency Order. Permission was granted and the weir was constructed shortly after and was made from aluminum I beams along with aluminum wing walls extending 4.5 feet on each side of the weir. The weir was designed to be adjustable depending on water levels. The width of the weir where water flows through was fixed at just under 12 feet. Recording gauges were placed just upstream and downstream of the weir in order to monitor water levels and monitoring began on August 30, 2010. The weir was subsequently removed by FWC who determined that it was ineffective in stopping the drainage of the creek upstream from the structure and was causing erosion and shoaling downstream.

In 2010, the FWC received an EPA Compliance Order notifying FWC that it was in violation of the Clean Water Act for discharging dredged and fill materials into waters of the United States within Cowbone Marsh without a permit. The EPA directed FWC to provide information to them to aid EPA "in reaching an appropriate enforcement resolution."

EPA also ordered FWC to submit a restoration plan to EPA. The plan would need to include: (a) stabilization of the discharge area; (b) removal of fill material; (c) restoration of impacted areas to original grade and contour; (d) replanting wetlands to pre-impact conditions; (e) a schedule for implementation, and; (f) submittal of long term monitoring and progress reports. The EPA Compliance Order required the FWC to begin implementation of the restoration plan within 30 days of EPA's approval and complete the restoration within 60 days of implementation. In 2011 EPA ordered the FWC to place five check dams within the cut area and to back fill the channel. The check dams were to be constructed with sandbags, plywood, coconut matting and pressure treated posts and each dam had ten foot wing walls on each side of the dam.

In 2011, DEP issued a permit to FWC to place six earthen check dams within the two mile cut in order to prevent the over draining of Cowbone Marsh. In 2012, the FWC applied to DEP for a modification of their original permit (issued 2011) and requested that they be able to backfill the channel cut with sand. DEP approved the modified permit to allow the backfilling of the two mile long cut with sand to be provided by dump trucks using an existing active borrow pit located just over a mile away near SR 27 to the southwest. A temporary access road would be built from the borrow pit, eastward along the top of the Herbert Hoover Dike and then northward to the southern end of the cut in Cowbone Marsh. That portion of the road which crossed through wetlands would be constructed of removable mats.

Immediately after this modified permit was issued, a Petition for an Administrative Hearing was submitted jointly by Save Our Rivers and the Environmental Coalition of Southwest Florida with the assistance of Earth Justice as one of the Appellants. The petition alleged that the proposed filling in of the cut would deny access to the petitioners to navigate through the Fisheating Creek Corridor. The Audubon Society disagreed with this and their official position was that the cut should be filled in to restore Cowbone Marsh back to its pre-cut condition. Eventually the Administrative Judge denied FWC's permit modification request to fill in the cut with sand. In 2014 the DEP issued its Consolidated Final Order denying the FWC's request to backfill the cut through Cowbone Marsh.

The Cowbone Marsh navigation project has been halted for now but the hydrology of Cowbone Marsh and Fisheating Creek has been altered somewhat from its pre-cut conditions. It is unclear if there will be a push to complete the canoe trail through Cowbone Marsh in the future or if the regulatory agencies will ever allow the cut to be completed. However, I don't believe the cut should be approved and completed unless further analysis shows it can be done without impacting the ecology of the creek.

As of now, there are too many potentially negative impacts which have been identified. These include changing the hydrology of the creek which could lower water levels even more; an increase in nutrients and sediment flowing downstream to Lake Okeechobee; high maintenance costs including the need for periodic herbicide spaying and mechanical removal of vegetation within the new channel cut; and increased boat traffic which could cause erosion to the Ft. Center archaeological site and disturb the wading bird populations including the nearby World Class swallow-tailed kite roost site. In addition, it should be kept in mind that as noted by the FWC, even if the navigation cut were completed, the route through Cowbone Marsh would only be passable during high water (usually July through September).

FLORIDA'S CONSERVATION PROGRAMS

The growth pressures beginning to be felt in Glades County and in the vicinity of the Fisheating Creek Ecosystem are also beginning to be felt throughout the Final Frontier from the Morman-owned Deseret Ranch south of Orlando, which is currently seeking to develop portions of its land, to the McDaniel Ranch south of Moore Haven which has already sold a portion of their ranch to a South Florida developer.

Fortunately, almost all of the Fisheating Creek Ecosystem is owned by one land owner, Lykes which eliminates the complexities of having to negotiate for conservation easements or fee simple acquisition with multiple owners. In addition, along with the 18,168 acres now owned by the State within the Expanded Corridor, and 41,696 acres protected by a conservation easement in Phase I of the Ecosystem, Lykes has indicated its possible willingness to sell additional conservation easements within the project boundary for the remaining 91,305 acres in Phases II, III, IV, and V and the 17,280 acre area south of C.R. 74, referred to as Future Potential Conservation Easement.

For many years, Floridians have enjoyed the benefits of living in a State which has had the most progressive series of land acquisition programs in the Nation. Florida's land acquisition programs have always received strong popular and political support and this is due to numerous factors.

Florida residents have also experienced the State's high population growth, averaging over 800 net residents per day and the accompanying loss of natural lands that they formally took for granted. Florida's natural environment has always been the foundation for its strong tourism industry. In addition, citizens and local governments are now aware that residential development typically does not usually pay for itself and must be subsidized by the tax payers. Empirical data refutes the long held claim by local governments and the development community that residential development is a windfall to local governments tax coffers. The costs to local governments to provide residential services such as central water and sewer, garbage, roads, schools, fire, and police is almost always more than the tax revenues received from residential development, especially so for urban sprawl residential development.

Historically the primary method to preserve conservation lands has been through either fee simple acquisition or acquisition of conservation easements with most funding now provided by the Florida Forever Program supplemented by funding from private organizations, such as the Nature Conservancy or the Trust for Public Lands.

122

The first of Florida's land acquisition programs began in 1963 with creation of the Land Acquisition Trust Fund (LATF) to purchase lands for parks and recreation areas. The LATF was funded through a five percent tax on outdoor equipment and clothing such as bathing suits. The fund generated about $1.5 million per year and lands for acquisition were selected and purchased by the Department of Natural Resources, now the DEP. In 1968 the tax used to fund the LATF was replaced with a $20 million recreation bond program paid for with funds from documentary stamp taxes paid on real estate transactions. Thus the development that was causing the loss of natural lands ended up being a source of funding to conserve natural lands. That program has since evolved over the years.

In 1972 the Florida Legislature passed the Land Conservation Act which created the Environmentally Endangered Lands Program (EEL) and later that same year the voters approved a referendum to authorize the sale of $200 million in bonds and another $40 million in recreation bonds. Debt service on both bond programs was paid for from proceeds of the documentary stamp tax on real estate taxes.

In 1979 the EEL program was expanded and replaced with the Conservation and Recreational Lands Program (CARL). Significantly, the CARL program called for a recurring revenue stream rather than a one time bond program and from 1979 to 1987 received its revenue from an excise tax on mineral extraction (mostly phosphate, oil, gas and other solid minerals). From 1987 to 1990 the CARL program also received funds from documentary stamp taxes. From 1979 to 1990 the CARL program protected 181,000 acres of conservation lands at a cost of $356 million.

In 1981 under the leadership of then Governor Bob Graham, the Save Our Coast (SOC) program was enacted by the Florida Legislature authorizing the sale of 275 million dollars in bonds for acquisition of lands along Florida's coasts. The SOC program was developed in response to the rapid loss of coastal lands to development and the recognition of the importance of undeveloped beaches to the State's valuable tourist industry. Ultimately the SOC program resulted in the purchase of 73,000 acres of coastal lands along 73 miles of protected coastline.

Also in 1981 under the leadership of Governor Graham, the Florida Legislature created the Water Management Lands Trust Fund, also known as the Save Our Rivers (SOR) program, which was also funded by proceeds of the documentary stamp tax on real estate transactions. The SOR funds were then distributed among the State's five Water Management Districts (WMD's) based on their respective populations to purchase lands in order to protect their surface and groundwater water resources. Together the five districts have purchased over 1.7 million acres of land.

In 1990 under then Governor Bob Martinez, the Florida Legislature created the Florida Preservation 2000 program (P2000) to be funded through sales of bonds in the amount of $300 million per year between 1990 and 2000 for a total of 3 billion dollars. The P2000 program was created through the realization that current funding was inadequate to meet the backlog of lands identified for purchase due to increased land values and the pace of development.

The P2000 funds were distributed as follows: (a) 50 percent to the CARL program; (b) 30 percent to the SOR program; (c) 10 percent to the Florida Communities Trust, a program created to help local government purchase historical or environmental lands; (d) 2.9 percent each to the Division of Recreation and Parks, Division of Forestry, and Game and Fish Commission, to purchase inholdings within State Parks, State Forests, and State owned Wildlife Management Areas respectively; and (e) 1.3 percent for recreational trails under the State Greenways and Trails Program. P2000 was a monumental success and ultimately protected almost 2 million acres of land for recreation and natural resource purposes.

In 1999, under the leadership of then Governor Lawton Chiles, the current successor to P2000 was enacted by the Legislature, and is known as the Florida Forever program. Florida Forever also authorized the sale of $300 million in bonds for ten years (2000 through 2010) but was to be distributed differently as follows: (a) 35 percent to the former CARL program; (b) 35 percent to the SOR program; (c) 24 percent to the Florida Communities Trust; (d) 1.5 percent each to the Division of Recreation and Parks, Division of Forestry, and Game and Fish Commission, to purchase inholdings within State Parks, State Forests, and State owned Wildlife Management Areas respectively; and (e) 1.5 percent for recreational trails. Florida Forever put more emphasis on urban and community parks, on water resources and supply, on conservation easements rather than fee simple acquisition, on restoration of ecosystems and control of exotic plants and animals, on land management, and on protection of historic and archaeological resources.

So far Florida Forever has preserved 638,600 acres of conservation lands and cultural resources. In addition, over 20 local governments have created their own land acquisition bond programs to purchase conservation lands and cultural resources within their respective counties or municipalities. The future of Florida Forever is uncertain due to Florida's recent budget constraints caused by the economic crisis including a severe reduction in property and sales taxes. As a result, the State's budget has been severely strained for the past few years and for the first time since its inception, funding for Florida Forever was not approved during the 2009 legislative session. Fortunately funding was approved for the 2010 fiscal year, but in a reduced amount of only $15 million, far less than the usual $300 million yearly maximum authorized for appropriation by the Florida Forever Program. In 2011 no funding was approved again and in 2012, the legislature allocated only $8.5 million to protect important water protection areas and conservation lands. In 2013 $50 million was funded. The future of the Florida Forever Program is uncertain, but there is hope that the program will remain alive and eventually regain its full funding once the economy turns around.

A current effort to ensure funding for the Florida Forever Program has been started by a coalition of conservation organization including Florida Wildlife Federation, Audubon Florida, 1000 Friends of Florida, The Nature Conservancy, the Trust For Public Lands, Sierra Club, and dozens of other local, state and national groups. The project is referred to as the Florida Water and Land Legacy and it recently obtained enough petition signatures for a constitutional amendment that will go on the Florida ballet in 2014 to provide guaranteed long term funding. Funding would be provided by dedicating one third of all documentary stamp revenues for restoration and conservation projects in Florida. If passed by the voters, it is estimated that the amendment will provide more than $5 billion for water and land conservation in Florida over the next ten years and $10 billion over the twenty-year life of the measure, all without any tax increase.

Even before the economic crisis, the environmental community has long acknowledged that, there will never be enough money to protect all of Florida's critical lands and waters through fee simple acquisition alone. More emphasis needs to be placed on the more economical acquisition of conservation easements and on creation of economically based incentive approaches to protect critical lands owned and managed by private individuals.

In addition to the Florida Forever Program, there are other State programs and policies which are helping to preserve Florida's last remaining natural areas. In 2008, 68 percent of the voters approved an amendment to the Florida State Constitution which will greatly benefit the State's efforts to preserve conservation lands on private ranches and farms. Known as the Land Conservation Amendment, this provision has two parts. The first part eliminates all property taxes on conservation lands where a perpetual conservation easement has been donated or sold. The second part reduces property taxes on conservation lands that are temporarily set aside for a shorter period of time. The lands with temporary easements must also be appraised by the local property tax appraiser based on their conservation use and not their potential use. The tax benefits became effective in the 2010 tax year. This new law was supported by the environmental community as well as Governor Crist and the Florida Chamber of Commerce. It is hoped that the amendment will provide an additional incentive to large landowners having lands with conservation values to donate or sell conservation easements to the State or other local governments.

Another fairly new Growth Management program which may provide a way to preserve some of the Final Frontier is the 2007 Rural Lands Stewardship program (RLS). The RLS program is a transfer of development rights program designed to promote protection of large rural landscapes. The RLS program was added to the State Growth Management Act as an option for large landowners who want to develop their property. Development credits are determined by the value of the land to be protected, known as the sending area. These credits are then transferred or sent to the receiving area where development is to occur. Sending and receiving areas must total at least 10,000 acres and can be in individual or multiple ownerships. RLS agreements must be approved by DCA as an amendment to the County Comprehensive Plan. Potential changes to this program may include requiring the receiving area to be located within or near existing urban areas to reduce urban sprawl and fragmentation of large rural landscapes.

The Adams Ranch in St. Lucie County is one of two parcels in the State that have received approval under the RLS program. On the surface, the Adams Ranch seems to be a good compromise between the desire for development and the preservation of native Florida habitats. However, some critics have subsequently questioned the wisdom of this RLS designation for Adams Ranch because the approved receiving area (development area) is in a rural area thereby contributing to sprawl.

There have also been questions about how much protection the Adams Ranch sending area will actually receive and whether it could potentially be cleared for more intensive agriculture than the low intensity cattle ranching that is currently practiced. There are already discussions about revising the RLS criteria to better address these types of issues such as requiring that receiving areas be located within an Urban Service Area. This program has potential and hopefully many of these issues will be resolved as time goes by and new projects apply for the RLS designation.

Another Growth Management program which is designed to help preserve some of Florida's farms and ranches is the Rural and Family Lands Protection Act (RFLPA) which was enacted by the Legislature in 2001 and is administered by the Florida Department of Agriculture and Consumer Services - Division of Forestry (FDACS). This program is also funded by the Florida Forever Program, however, unlike the Florida Forever program which focuses on the protection of the natural environment, the RFLPA focuses on maintaining an agricultural land base in Florida. This program was designed to meet three specific needs: (a) to protect valuable agricultural lands. (b) to create conservation easements which will ensure sustainable agricultural practices and provide reasonable protection of the environment without interfering with agricultural operations that could put the economic viability of these operations at risk, and (c) to protect natural resources, not as a primary purpose, but in conjunction with economic viable operations.

The RFLPA program recognizes that landowners of ranch and forest lands generally have a healthy respect for Florida's natural resources as evident by their ability to maintain some of the best remaining examples of intact ecosystems, natural communities, and wild habitats in Florida. By focusing on agricultural lands with important natural resource attributes, the simultaneous benefits of a healthy natural environment can be achieved without adversely impacting agricultural productivity. The Florida Forever Act has allocated an annual distribution of up to $10.5 million, or 3.5% of the total $300 million allocated annually for the RFLPA program. Researchers have determined that many of the remaining important natural habitats are located on ranch lands in central and south Florida so perhaps the Legislature should consider distributing a larger share of the Florida Forever budget to this important program.

It is now acknowledged that Central Florida's low intensity cattle ranches provide more than just cow calf production. Unlike high intensity grazing systems which provide high food production but little in the way of ecosystem services, many of Florida's low intensity cattle ranches complement and preserve their natural systems and provide a heterogeneous landscape with a host of ecosystem services which can be simply described as "the benefits people obtain from ecosystems." In addition, the remaining unprotected conservation lands within the Final Frontier identified within the Florida Ecological Greenways Network (FEGN) are found primarily on these cattle ranches. Cattle ranches represent some of the most important remaining parcels of contiguous native habitat in the State. These ranches conserve the region's biodiversity necessary for many of Florida's remaining threatened and endangered species.

As a result, a new concept is being discussed by State and local environmental organizations which is referred to as "Ecosystem Services." These services can include the provision of food, fiber, and fuel; preservation of cultural and natural heritage; water purification and supply, climate regulation and carbon sequestering, opportunities for recreation and education, maintenance of soil fertility; maintenance of biological diversity; and preservation of threatened and endangered species. Federal, State, and local governments as well as conservation organizations are all beginning to consider developing innovative programs that will pay ranchers for these services. The degree of ecosystem services provided depends on the management practices practiced by each individual rancher.

In 2005 this concept was taken a step further through initiation of the Florida Ranchlands Environmental Services Project (FRESP), a program that would pay ranchers in the Northern Everglades to provide environmental services with a goal specifically of water retention and phosphorous load reduction into Lake Okeechobee and the Everglades. This is a voluntary program that will pay ranchers to manage their surface waters north of Lake Okeechobee to reduce the amount of water required to be stored in the lake. This will improve the lake's ecosystems which have been stressed by high water and will also reduce harmful discharges of freshwater into the St. Lucie and Caloosahatchee River Estuaries. In addition, the stored water on these ranches could provide much needed water during times of drought. Finally, the water retained on these ranches would help meet the water quality goals for Lake Okeechobee by capturing and holding phosphorus prior to releasing the water into the lake.

A side benefit of this program will be the economic incentives for ranchers to stay in business rather than sell the land for possibly more intensive agricultural uses or urban development which could further degrade surface water quality entering Lake Okeechobee. In addition the land would remain on the tax roles and continue to provide property taxes to the local government.

The pilot program is a collaborative effort by eight ranchers in the Okeechobee watershed, the World Wildlife Fund, FDACS, SFWMD, DEP, USDA, the University of Florida, and the MacArthur Agro-ecology Research Center with funding provided by various public and private agencies. Of the eight participating ranches, four pilot projects were constructed and are now operational.

One of these pilot projects is located in Glades County on the Lykes Ranch just north of the proposed Fisheating Creek Ecosystem Project boundary.

Known as the West Waterhole Marsh, it consists of a 2,400 acre pasture which is surrounded by a dike and contains wetlands and wet prairie located south of S.R. 70 and west of Indian Prairie Canal (C-40). Water is pumped from the C-40 canal into the detention reservoir in order to provide freeze protection to the adjacent citrus grove during the winter. The water is discharged back into the C-40 canal after treatment where it flows southeast another 13 or so miles before discharging into Lake Okeechobee. Recent water quality tests conducted during an 11 week pilot project showed that the detention area had removed 3.3 metric tons of total phosphorous as well as 39,763 pounds of nitrogen.

The pilot projects will continue through 2011 and the ultimate goal of the program is to create a new product for ranchers known as water management services which will generate a new revenue source for ranchers, many of which have small profits margins. Ranchers will enter into fixed contracts ranging in terms of between five and twenty years and ranchers will be required to provide annual documentation, subject to rainfall, that they have met the terms of the contract to provide water management services.

A host of other existing Federal and State tax incentives are also in effect to encourage land owners to preserve the conservation value on their lands. Federal income tax deductions can be made for donating conservation easements on environmental lands, for costs associated with conservation expenditures, and on revenue from lands used to support natural habitats. Recent changes to Federal income tax laws have increased incentives for donating conservation easements including a deduction of up to half of adjusted gross income in any given year, a deduction of up to 100% of adjusted income for certain qualifying farmers and ranchers, and deductions can be taken for as long as 16 years for qualifying donations. Also, certain qualifying farmers and ranchers can deduct all or some of Federal or State cost/share conservation payments from their gross income.

The Federal Tax Payer Relief Act also provides an incentive for a landowner to put a conservation easement on his land by excluding up to 40 percent of the land's value from the taxable estate. Caveats include a maximum tax exclusion of $500,000 and the program is available only to landowners with easements that reduce the fair market value of the property by at least 30 percent. The law also allows capital gains taxes to be reduced for land that is sold with a donated conservation easement. Twenty five percent of the value of the land having a conservation easement can be excluded from paying capital gains taxes.

Florida's past attempts to control growth, preserve agricultural lands and prevent fragmentation of important wildlife habitats through land use regulations have been only partially effective. However, as the preceding examples demonstrate, the State and Federal Government have been doing a much better job in developing incentive programs to encourage ranchers to preserve their land while also compensating them financially. In addition, numerous interest groups and State leaders have also begun to provide suggestions for ways to improve growth management and preserve Florida's vanishing agricultural lands and wildlife habitats. Recommendations include making farmland protection a priority including adding provisions to the Florida Growth Management Act and trying to balance regulatory and non-regulatory regulations, increasing funding for agricultural incentives programs, and also acquisition, research and public education.

Glades County may play the most critical role in helping to preserve the remaining lands within the Fisheating Creek Ecosystem as well as other identified SHCA lands through implementation of their Comprehensive Plan and Land Development Regulations. Currently the county Future Land Use Map designates most of the lands within the Fisheating Creek Ecosystem as either Conservation or Agriculture. More intensive Future Land Use designations are associated with existing developed areas including the only incorporated municipality of Moore Haven (which has their own Future Land Use Map), and the unincorporated communities of Lakeport, Buckhead Ridge, Muse Village north of LaBelle, Ortona, Venus and Palmdale.

Fortunately Glades County has been proactive in discussions about the future of the County. In 2006 the Florida Heartland Rural Economic Development Initiative obtained a grant from the Florida Department of Community Affairs to conduct a "Glades County Visioning Process." The focus of the process was to have Glades County citizens identify what was important to them individually and then to develop vision priorities as a group. The process was supported by a steering committee composed of local government officials as well as business interests, including two representatives from Lykes.

Following the process, funding sources were identified to address the vision priorities by providing technical assistance to: (a) Help complete updates to the Glades County and City of Moore Haven Comprehensive Plans; (b) Create a Natural Resources Preservation Plan, and (c) Design, infrastructure and marketing of a business park.

The vision included recommendations that open space and natural resources be protected; increase economic development to boost the economy and provide quality jobs and supporting government services, and; increase education and health care services for a growing population. Residents also want to help set development standards before major growth occurs. The process also developed a set of Goals and Objectives which included a desire for development that enhances the quality of life while also maintaining the rural character of the county and preserving the county's natural resources.

Other suggestions included limiting what was termed "dumping ground" development such as prisons, landfills, and toxic waste processing facilities. Planners have long referred to these types of uses as LULU's an acronym for Locally Undesirable Land Uses and the desire not to have these uses near residential areas as NIMBY or Not In My Back Yard. These are uses which are necessary but which most people do not want to be located near to where they live. Power plants, tactical para-military training complexes, and large scale mining would fall under that category as well.

The Vision also stated that Glades County should promote development which is compact and located around existing population centers and which is also economically diverse and mixed. According to Enterprise Florida, the four largest private employers currently in Glades County are the Moore Haven Prison which uses private security employing approximately 219 persons, Lykes which employs approximately 100 person, Brighton Seminole Reservation Bingo which employs approximately 80 persons and Glades Electric Utility which employs approximately 65 person.

The Vision also recommended that Glades County develop its natural, recreational and historic resources for residents to use and to attract tourists from the large nearby coastal communities. One of the priorities related to this desire for more eco-tourism was to promote Fisheating Creek as a world class 52 mile long canoe trail which should be regionally governed. Also related to Fisheating Creek, the Vision Process recommended that the old Cypress Knee Museum created and run by the late Tom Gaskins in Palmdale be restored as a museum. The Vision suggested that Glades County promote the acquisition of conservation areas by the Florida Forever Program as well as the purchase of conservation easements to preserve agricultural and conservation areas. Related to this the Vision Process also suggested that the County promote green spaces and wildlife corridors. All of these recommendations are to be commended.

MY TIME ON THE CREEK

Up until this Chapter I have focused on providing information on the unique and abundant natural resources of the Fisheating Creek region as well as some of the growth challenges facing this special area. I think this story would be incomplete without including some of the personal experiences I have enjoyed on the creek over the years with my father and brother. This book is dedicated to my father Alex who passed away in August of 2010 at the age of 88. Alex took the time to take my brother Randall and me on many camping, hunting and fishing trips when we were young including many trips to Fisheating Creek. The book is also dedicated to my brother Randall who passed away in December of 2013 at the age of 59 after a courageous fight with cancer and who was my fishing and canoeing buddy on many trips to Fisheating Creek over the years.

In the summer of 1968 bd (before Disney), my family moved to Fort Lauderdale from sleepy Orlando. After adjusting to our new life in Ft. Lauderdale, my father Alex, and my brother Randall and I soon discovered that there was a State Wildlife Management Area called Fisheating Creek located less than a two hour drive from our home and that it allowed camping during the hunting season. Alex decided to take us there during the 1969 Christmas Holiday season since he had some time off from work and Randall and I would also have some holiday time off from school. We bought a new wall tent that was large enough for all three of us to sleep in and which was made of heavy canvas (back before lightweight nylon became the norm for tents). We were going to go camping and try our luck at turkey hunting. Randall and I were excited and ready for this new adventure. We were already experienced hunters having been dove and duck hunting numerous times with our dad starting at the ages of 11 and 12 respectively.

We left for the creek heading west from Ft. Lauderdale on S.R. 84, now part of I-75. At that time S.R. 84 was only two lanes all the way to Naples and the City of Weston in western Ft. Lauderdale did not exist. Weston was incorporated in 1996 and has a current population of over 62,000 person and sprawls across 17,000 acres of land on the south side of S.R. 84 and east of U.S. 27. In 1969 the Weston tract was still part of the Everglades and driving west along S.R. 84 it was common to see air boaters accessing the north side of the tract from the south side of S.R. 84.

Once we reached U.S. 27 we headed north towards Lake Okeechobee and at that time U.S. 27 was also two lanes and was bordered most of the way by canals, guardrails and Australian Pines. This was a deadly stretch of road and you had to pay attention because faster drivers were always trying to pass slower drivers or agricultural vehicles and head-on collisions were common. Somewhere in the vicinity of Lake Okeechobee, U.S. 27 became four lanes and the ride became safer and more relaxing. As it is today, Lake Okeechobee was not visible from the highway and all you could see was the large dike (Herbert Hoover) which surrounds the lake. The ride seemed to take forever as it passed through mile after mile of sugarcane fields and an occasional agricultural town including South Bay, Lake Harbor, Clewiston and finally Moore Haven.

About five miles west of Moore Haven, U.S. 27 takes a northwest turn as it heads towards the little community of Palmdale where Fisheating Creek crosses under U.S. 27. About 5 miles from Palmdale where U.S. 27 crosses the Seaboard Coastline railroad, the treeline of Fisheating Creek became visible off to the north. At this point the scenery began to change from cane fields and improved pasture to native pasture consisting of saw palmetto "prairies" and there was still a frontier feel to the land. Off to the northeast, across several miles of pasture and prairie lands, there was a clear view of the treeline associated with Fisheating Creek, especially some very tall cypress trees. The treeline runs south and west for five or six miles towards Palmdale. Forty years ago the tree line of Fisheating Creek was more visible and it appears that many more oak trees are now growing in the prairies obstructing the view.

My first impression of this treeline off in the distant horizon was of a place remote, wild and beautiful. Being a teenager with a strong imagination, I also imagined that every oak hammock near the creek had a flock of wild turkeys walking through it. As we drove towards Palmdale the tree line of the creek bottom northeast of the highway got closer and closer finally merging with the road as we crossed over the creek on the US 27 bridge.

We were now in Palmdale. Not far past the Fisheating Creek bridge on the left was the hunt check station for the Wildlife Management Area. At that time, the Management Area was huge and encompassed over 75,000 acres west of U.S. 27 including the creek bottom north to the Glades/Highlands County line. It also included a large triangular tract of land known as Mizell Island between SR 29 on the east, C.R. 731 on the west, and C.R. 74 on the north where only Spring Turkey hunting was allowed. There were also public campsites on the east side of U.S. 27 along the north side of the creek where hunting was not allowed.

After checking in with a bored looking man at the hunt check station, which was little more than a small wooden shack large enough to hold one person, we headed west on a wide dirt road towards one of the designated hunt camps in the interior of the WMA near the creek. After driving about four miles through a vast area of palmetto prairie the road took a sharp S turn to the right and then to the left where it crossed a small unnamed tributary to the creek. We continued on for about two more miles and then took a smaller dirt road off to the left which ran south toward the creek bottom for about a mile where we then came to the campground. It was a beautiful area located at the edge of the creek bottom with many large live oaks and a park like understory where many tents were pitched along the length of the hammock but with enough room to have privacy and space to spread out. The creek itself was located south about a half mile through the swamp so there was no direct access to it.

We spent a couple of days at the camp site and spent time hunting in the creek bottom as well as driving the main road in the WMA but saw no turkeys. However we did see quite a few large healthy looking quail running across the dirt roads and into the palmettos during our drives around the WMA. Randall and I were hooked on Fisheating Creek and could not wait to return.

On a subsequent trip to Fisheating Creek, after passing through the same check station, we headed west again and soon discovered that this time the dirt road was in terrible shape due to dry conditions and was also heavily rutted from hunting vehicle use. Randall was driving our dark green Vega which was only two wheel drive and I was in the front seat with my dad in the back. Randall had to drive extremely fast in order to keep our momentum and not sink into the deep sandy ruts.

Randall drove like a wild man for about five miles through the palmetto prairie until finally finding the small campsite we were looking for. However, when we got there we discovered that it was occupied by three "rough" looking characters who seemed to be living there permanently. We had a bad feeling about the situation and decided to head back out to Palmdale and camp at the eastern campground east of U.S. 27 on the north bank of Fisheating Creek. So the wild ride we had getting to the campsite was repeated as we headed the five or so miles back to U.S. 27 in Palmdale.

The roads were better on the east campgrounds and even though we could not hunt there, the scenery was excellent and we had a campsite directly on the creek. That night the temperature quickly plummeted and the wind picked up and by morning it was in the 30's which is cold for South Central Florida. We had thin south Florida style sleeping bags and no thermal underwear and we spent a long cold sleepless night but it was a great adventure.

On another occasion we decided that we would try to access the upstream portion of the creek from the bridge at C.R. 731 near Venus and camp out for one night. I think this was one of my crazy ideas. We had a small 12 foot aluminum boat with a 7 h.p. Mercury outboard and the three of us piled into that little boat with all our camping gear and headed south down the creek. We got about a mile down the creek and began to have second thoughts. For one thing our car was parked right on the side of the road in a very desolate area; second, the land along the creek in that area was outside the WMA and privately owned, and thirdly the creek in that area was very swampy and we did not see any dry land to camp on. We ended up returning to the car and after packing up we drove back to Palmdale and again camped at the campground east of U.S. 27 at a beautiful campsite directly on the creek under some beautiful live oaks.

The next morning we decided to venture down the creek to see how far we could get. After paddling for awhile, the creek turned towards the north and northeast and became braided into numerous shallow channels. We decided to get out on one of the small islands formed by the braided creek. As soon as we got out of the boat we heard a group of turkeys coming towards us through the trees so we decided to crouch down and hide to see if they would come closer. The turkeys flew across the west channel of the creek onto the island and walked across it to within a few yards of us. They apparently never saw us as they continued across the island. When they reached the far side of the island they flew across the east channel of the creek and continued on their way.

In the spring of 1975 Randall and I decided we were going to take our aluminum motorboat and go up Fisheating Creek to camp at the Fort Center Indian Mound a few miles upstream from S.R. 78 west Lake Okeechobee. We also planned to try some turkey hunting since it was Spring Gobbler season. We arrived at the S.R. 78 boat ramp on Fisheating Creek located just south of Lakeport and loaded up our boat with all our camping gear. We also had my 16 gauge Ithaca pump shotgun (which I got as a Christmas present in 1966 and still have) along with some #6 birdshot and a cedar box turkey caller.

We headed up the creek and because this was Spring, typically the driest time of the year, the creek was very shallow. We had to get out of the boat numerous times and walk along the bank while pushing from behind or pulling it with a rope tied to the bow. We did not know it at that time but the term used to describe this procedure is called "lining" the boat. Lining

135

has been around since boats were invented and is usually required when water is either too shallow, or currents and/or wind are too strong.

We were quite far up the creek and miles from the highway surrounded by pasture and prairie and had gotten about half way to the Fort Center site when we noticed a pick up truck heading across the prairie straight towards us from the southeast. When the truck reached us, the two men inside who looked like classic Florida cowboys, got out and asked us what we were doing. We told them we were going to camp at Fort Center for a couple of nights. They explained that they worked for Lykes and that we were on Lykes private property and that Fort Center was also owned by Lykes. They asked us if we had any guns and we told them we had a shotgun for protection (we conveniently omitted the fact that we also had a turkey caller and had planned to hunt for turkeys). They told us that we could camp at Fort Center but that we would not be allowed to hunt. We agreed to their request and thanked them, then continued on up the creek as they drove off back to the southeast. Even though we canceled our plans to hunt, we thought that they would not mind if we used the turkey caller to see if we could call up a gobbler just for the fun of it.

We arrived at the Fort Center Site and pitched our tent on a small bluff with a beautiful view overlooking the creek and the vast open areas of the floodplain marsh to the north, east and west. Directly behind us was a forest of live oaks and just to the east was a mound and ditch work from the old Fort Center Mound Complex.

The Fort Center archaeological site consists of mounds, ponds, circular ditches, and linear embankments built along a mile of creek front over at least 2000 years ago by people of the Belle Glade culture. The Belle Glade culture was an archaeological culture which existed from about 1000 BCE to about 1700 in the area surrounding Lake Okeechobee and the Kissimmee River Valley. Professor William Sears of Florida Atlantic University excavated the site with help from students from the University of Florida and Colgate University and their work spanned a six year period between 1966 and 1971.

The site is now owned by the State and hikers can hike to Fort Center from the nearby FWC field station located to the east at the end of Banana Grove Road off S.R. 78. However, at the time of Sear's excavation work, the site was owned by Lykes who allowed Sears access to the site as well as providing him with funding and equipment in support of the project. Sears published a book about his research in 1982 entitled *Fort Center: An Archaeological Site in the Lake Okeechobee Basin.* Sears believed that corn

Randall at Ft. Center campsite – 1975

Randall passing Ft. Center Mound – 1975

Author in oak hammock at Ft. Center - 1975

pollen found at the site indicates that the Belle Glade people grew corn. If this is true, then Fort Center would be one of the earliest, if not the earliest, example of agriculture in the pre-Columbian Eastern United States. Sears theorized that the ditches were dug to drain the soil for corn.

At the site, human remains were found along with the remnants of a wooden platform decorated with wooden carvings of wildlife including life-size cats, a bear, foxes, eagles, and wading birds. Other objects were preserved in the muck at the bottom of the pond including a wooden carving of an otter running with a fish in its mouth. The site, listed in the National Register of Historic Places, was still occupied, although there was no evidence of agriculture, when the Europeans arrived in the 16th and 17th centuries.

Randall and I got up early the next morning and while preparing breakfast we heard a turkey gobbling every few minutes about a quarter of a mile to the south of our campsite. We decided to see if we could call him in, so after breakfast we began walking to the south and east toward the sound of

138

the turkey. We took our caller but left the shotgun in the tent. When we got a little closer, I decided to try the caller to see what would happen. I shook the caller and it made the sound of a male gobbling. Right away we heard the gobbler respond to us and shortly after that he gobbled again but this time he was closer and we know he would be able to see us soon. We hid behind some palmettos and used the caller again when suddenly we saw the turkey running out from the trees into the clearing in front of us.

The turkey was a large mature adult and when he got to the clearing he began to strut while arching his wings and fanning out his tail feathers and his head was a bright reddish/orange. He was putting on quite a show and we were surprised that we had actually fooled him since we had never called in a gobbler before. After a while he became suspicious and may have caught a glimpse us because he eventually worked his way back to where he came from and we did not see or hear him again after that. We had a great camping trip at Fort Center and other than the two cowboys that stopped us, we did not see another person on the creek the entire time.

On another occasion in the early 70's my father decided to take Randall me duck hunting at Lake Okeechobee. We arrived at the S.R. 78 boat ramp at Fisheating Creek not long after sunrise after driving from Ft. Lauderdale. We loaded up our aluminum boat, cranked up the motor and headed down Fisheating Creek towards Lake Okeechobee. As we approached the Lake the creek opened up into a an area called Fisheating Bay, a popular spot to hunt ducks. We threw out some decoys and tried our best to camouflage the boat with camouflage cloth. We saw several flocks of ducks but none of them got close enough for a shot so after about an hour we decided to go back up Fisheating Creek past the S.R. 78 bridge and try to jump shoot some puddle ducks in the pastures and marshes of Cowbone Marsh.

After motoring up the creek for a few miles, my dad dropped me off and he and Randall headed back downstream to try another spot and they agreed to pick me up at the same spot in about an hour. I spent that hour enjoying the solitude and the scenery as I walked around the pastures and marshes looking for puddle ducks in the numerous small U shaped oxbow ponds adjacent to the creek. These oxbow ponds, also referred to as oxbow lakes, were originally part of the old creek channel but became isolated when a wide meander from the main stem of the creek eventually became cut off, thereby forming the small isolated ponds. An aerial view of this lower section of the creek west of SR 78 reveals dozens of these oxbow ponds which provide excellent resting and feeding areas for puddle ducks as well as wading birds and other wildlife.

I saw several flocks of Green Winged Teal flying by in the distance but they never got close enough for a clean shot. When it was time to meet up with my dad and brother I began heading back to the pick up spot but continued to scan the horizon for ducks and to look for any potholes that may be holding some ducks. As I walked scanning the horizon I was not focusing on the ground when all of a sudden the ground gave way and I was suddenly in cold water up to my neck. I managed to keep my head above water as well as hold onto my gun and was able to scurry back up the bank and out onto dry land.

Once I got over the shock of what had happened I realized that I had walked into a small but deep oxbow pond that was completely covered in duck weed which caused it to blend in perfectly with the surrounding pasture. I heard my dad and brother coming up the creek and when they saw me soaking wet and covered in duck weed they asked me what happened. We laughed about it later but I was embarrassed about it and was glad I had not lost my gun in the dunking.

In the winter of 1989 I drove south from Jacksonville to visit with my parents who had recently retired to Vero Beach. After leaving my parents house I headed towards Ft. Lauderdale to visit my brother Randall and his family. When I left Ft. Lauderdale to head home I decided to take a side trip around the south side of Lake Okeechobee and on to Palmdale and Fisheating Creek for old times sake. Shortly after passing through Moore Haven on U.S 27, I started thinking about the old hand made wooden signs that could be seen along the north side of the highway for years and which advertised the now closed Cypress Knee Museum in Palmdale also called Cypress Kneeland. These signs were made by the late Tom Gaskins, who began homesteading on Fisheating Creek in Palmdale in the late 1930's and then opened the Museum in 1951. The Highway Beautification Act resulted in the signs removal in the 1990's and even though they may not have been beautiful, they were very folksy and humorous and a part of Americana and Old Florida.

Tom had a fascination with cypress knees and he had a collection of uniquely shaped knees that he harvested from the creek bottom near the Museum and which he demonstrated and sold at his museum. Many of the knees had unusual shapes and some resembled people or animals. He was know to be somewhat eccentric and was known to go barefoot most of the time and supposedly would jog up to five miles every day through the swamp in his bare feet. He made an appearance on the old Tonight Show with Johnny Carson as well as Jay Leno discussing his cypress knees and the Museum. He also displayed his cypress knees at the 1939-40 World's

Fair in New York.

In all the years my dad, Randall and I had passed by the Museum on the way to Fisheating Creek, we had never stopped, so I decided I would stop in to see what it was all about. I parked in the Museum lot which was devoid of cars and made my way into the dimly lit museum which smelled of cypress and had a collection of cypress knees everywhere. It was very quiet and I was wondering if I should say something to get someone's attention when all of a sudden Tom Gaskins walks in from the back of the store and introduces himself. He was very friendly and we shook hands and introduced ourselves. He spent some time telling me about his Museum and he seemed very proud of it. I was honored to be talking to him since I had heard about him for most of my life and respected his love of nature and his independent streak.

After talking for about 15 minutes I did not want to overstay my welcome so I thanked him and as I prepared to leave, he said he wanted to give me one of his cypress knees. He picked out a beautiful knee about twelve inches tall and which he had polished and hollowed out from the bottom to make it lighter (I still have that knee today). I thanked him again and as we walked outside I asked him if I could take his picture. He said he would be happy to and then he asked me if I wanted to take a picture of him standing on his head. I was surprised by this question, especially since the man was about 80 years old at that time (although he looked very fit), but I agreed knowing it would be a great picture that I could talk about for years to come. He then got down on the ground, kicked his feet up in the air and was on a three point headstand in a flash. Some of his pencils he had in his front pocket protector fell out and I snapped the picture. I took another self timed picture of us standing together and I cherish those photos to this day.

Tom Gaskins passed away on May 2, 1998 at the age of 89 in a nursing home in Miami and the Museum subsequently closed in June of 2000. His son, Tom Gaskins Jr. is attempting to move the Museum to another site and to renovate it.

After many years away from Fisheating Creek, with our time spent getting an education, working on our careers, getting married and for Randall, raising a family, Randall and I decided in 2007 to go canoeing on Fisheating Creek for old times sake. We would be using my old trusty 16 foot Mohawk canoe (which I have owned now for almost 30 years) to do some fishing and exploring along the creek.

Author and Tom Gaskins – 1989

We reserved a motel room in Lakeport and met there on a friday morning, he driving north from Ft, Lauderdale and me driving south from Jacksonville where I lived for over 20 years until moving to St. Augustine in 2010. As soon as we finished checking into our motel, we decided to drive to the lake located directly behind the motel and which could be reached by driving down the end of Herbert Hoover Dike which ran alongside the Harney Pond Canal In Lakeport. When we reached the lake we were shocked to see that it was the lowest we had ever seen it due to the extreme drought occurring in South Florida at that time. Much of the lake bottom was exposed and where there was water it was very shallow. We were at the lake during one of the worst droughts ever recorded in South Florida. After eating lunch we headed south towards the Fisheating Creek boat ramp on S.R. 78. We loaded the canoe with fishing gear and clamped on a small 3 h.p. Sears Gamefisher outboard to get up the creek a little faster. We intended to go at least as far as Fort Center for old times sake since the last we were there had been the 1975 camping trip, 32 years prior.

However we quickly realized that due to the drought, the creek was also low and it would be a long difficult trip to get to Fort Center. We were not nearly as young as we were when we first visited Fort Center. We went as far as an old bridge crossing about a quarter of a mile upstream of the S.R. 78 where the old pilings could be easily seen due to the low water. We ended up fishing around the S.R. 78 bridge and after that went down the creek closer to Fisheating Bay. That night we noticed several large fires out in Lake Okeechobee a few miles southeast of Lakeport. Lake Okeechobee was actually on fire and those fires burned during the entire two days we were there.

The next day we drove to Curry Island just south of Lakeport which is formed by Fisheating Creek to the north, Lake Okeechobee to the east, and the large canal along the north side of Herbert Hoover Dike to the south and west. Much of the marshland around the perimeter of Curry Island was exposed and had been burned to the ground. We then headed to Palmdale with the canoe to do some fishing and exploring since we had not been there for many years as well.

We launched the canoe from the boat ramp in the Fisheating Creek Campground which was crowded with campers and we headed down the creek passing under the railroad bridge and then the U.S. 27 bridge into the small unnamed lake east of the bridge. At the far end of the lake we caught and released several small bass and then we headed out of the lake and down the creek which immediately became very shallow. The creek was only few inches deep in many spots and we had to get out and push or pull it until we got to a deeper pool of water. We got as far as the bridge pilings where the old Main Street bridge used to cross the creek and after fishing for awhile we began our return upstream since the creek looked too low to continue downstream.

As soon as we started back we hit a canoe traffic jam of at least ten canoes many of which were being dragged and pulled by boy scouts. There was a sea of young people and canoes everywhere trying to maneuver past each other. Once we got back to the unnamed lake east of the U.S. 27 bridge the crowd subsided but it made us realize how popular the creek had become since we had last been here almost 35 years previously. I guess we shouldn't have been surprised because after all there are now over 7 million people living within a two hour drive of Fisheating Creek.

After canoeing at Fisheating Creek we decided to try our luck fishing in Lake Hicpochee since we had never seen it and we would pass near it on the way back to Lakeport. Once we reached Moore Haven we drove south along a two lane road running along the west side of the Okeechobee Waterway. The road eventually dead ended at a public boat ramp on the lake a few miles south of Moore Haven. We fished for a couple of hours but didn't catch anything. However, it was a nice cool day with a strong breeze so we at least enjoyed the weather and the scenery.

143

Randall at Ft. Center 2010

Author at Ft. Center 2010

Randall downstream from Palmdale – 2010

Heading back upstream towards Palmdale – 2010

On a subsequent trip in 2010, on a beautiful fall morning, Randall and I met at the Fisheating Creek boat ramp on S.R. 78 just south of Lakeport to spend the weekend canoeing and fishing on the creek as well as in Fisheating Bay in Lake Okeechobee. I drove down from St. Augustine and Randall drove up U.S. 27 from Ft. Lauderdale. Our goal that morning was to try to make it up the creek approximately nine miles to the willow swamp where the FWC had attempted to cut a channel earlier in the summer through Cowbone Marsh. On the way, we also planned to eat lunch at Ft. Center approximately four miles upstream from our put in, where we had last camped almost 35 years prior. I had been watching the gage height data for Lakeport and Palmdale on the internet for the previous week and we knew the creek level was falling fast and would soon be too shallow to navigate even by canoe.

We clamped on the trusty old 3 hp Sears Gamefisher to help us make it up the creek and it cranked right up even though it was at least 25 years old and had not been used for over a year. We also fastened a bright orange bicycle flag to the end of a ten foot pole and mounted it to the stern in case any airboats coming down the creek would see us coming and slow down. We were making good time and we admired the large number of yellow wild flowers growing along the banks as well as all over the lower creek. We saw lots of Black Angus cattle along and in the creek as well as numerous alligators. We fished just upstream of the S.R. 78 bridge the old bridge pilings cross the creek and then continued on up the creek. After passing the FWC Field Office on our left, the water began to get shallow in spots and several times we had to cut the motor and paddle until we found deeper water again. The creek became shallower as we headed upstream and after about an hour we could see the oak hammocks and bluff where Ft. Center was located. We pulled over to eat lunch under an isolated oak tree and while studying our aerial photo we realized that the campsite where we had camped 35 years prior was another few bends upstream.

We noticed that in the 35 years we had been away, the area seemed to have grown up with more oak trees and there were fewer open areas where the mounds were located. We finally saw the heavily treed area on our left where we had camped on the bluff all those years ago. It was hardly recognizable due to all the trees. We got out and walked up the bluff and found a kiosk which displayed information on the Belle Glade people that William Sears had described in his survey of the mounds in the early 1970's. The view here of the creek and the prairies and marshes beyond it to the north and west is even more beautiful than we remembered 35 years ago. We spent some time poking around the creek and noticed several small shards of pottery which were as Sears had described them, smooth and dark

146

(almost black) in color. At this point the creek was only about a foot deep and we realized that we could not go any farther upstream with the canoe.

So after a 35 year reunion with Ft. Center, we headed back downstream, knowing there was a good chance we would never return to this spot but we would always remember it as a special place and are thankful that it is now under state ownership for future Floridians to enjoy. About half way back to S.R. 78 we saw a mature Southern bald eagle flying over the creek trying to dodge a flock of angry crows. The eagle finally decided to hold his ground and landed in a dead tree next to the creek which looked like a spot he had used regularly. The crows were still harassing him when we rounded another bend and lost site of him. We spent the rest of the afternoon fishing in lower Fisheating Creek and Fisheating Bay in Lake Okeechobee.

The following day we decided to go to Palmdale and canoe downstream to see how far we could get, knowing the water level would be very low. We first attempted to launch at the Main Street put in on the east side of U.S. 27 at the south end of Main Street. The old canal adjacent to the Main Street which used to cross over Fisheating Creek east of U.S. 27 can be used for access during high water. However we discovered that the canal was dry and only had stagnant water in a few low spots so access to the creek was not possible. After launching from the Fisheating Creek Outpost we traveled downstream past the railroad bridge and the U.S. 27 bridge. The scenery was fantastic and after about a mile we reached a spot where the only way to keep going was to duck under a low overhanging oak tree. Once we passed that spot we saw no other canoes. Unfortunately the creek was again very low but we made it downstream about two more miles before deciding to eat lunch and turn around, knowing that the trip back upstream would not be quite as easy as going downstream.

After our trip to Palmdale we returned for an early dinner in Lakeport where we had fried catfish caught from Lake Okeechobee, which according to our waitress, had been caught by fishermen using trot lines since use of nets had been outlawed years before. We then headed back towards our hotel and watched the sun go down as we fished along the banks of Harney Pond Canal where it meets Lake Okeechobee. It was a beautiful way to end the day and our weekend in Florida's Final Frontier. It also turned out to be the last trip Randall and I would take to Fisheating Creek together because he passed away from cancer a few years later. The pictures I took of that trip will always be a special reminder of my brother and the times we spent together in the great outdoors of Florida, especially at Fisheating Creek.

147

CONCLUSIONS

The Fisheating Creek region is part of Florida's Final Frontier and it is strategically located between Lake Okeechobee to the east, the Lake Wales Ridge to the northeast, the State-owned Babcock Webb Wildlife Management Area and Babcock Ranch to the west, and the State-owned Okaloacoochee Slough and Big Cypress Swamp to the south. In addition, the Florida Ecological Greenways Network has identified the Fisheating Creek/Highlands Hammock corridor as a Critical Linkage to the north of Fisheating Creek. This linkage connects the Fisheating Creek Ecosystem to an area within Highlands County as far north as Highlands Hammock State Park which is known to be the habitat for a sub-population of Florida black bear.

An astounding 89 percent of the Fisheating Creek area has been designated by the FWC as Strategic Habitat Conservation Area (SHCA) for one or more listed species of animals and essential to providing some of the state's rarest animals, plants, and natural communities with the land base necessary to sustain populations into the future. The strategic location of the Fisheating Creek Ecosystem coupled with its abundance of important wildlife habitats make this special place vitally important to the long-term welfare of the Florida panther, Florida black bear, swallow-tailed kite, Florida sandhill crane, crested caracara along with numerous other species native to the region. I would hope that the SFWMD reconsiders their plan to flood Nicodemus Slough, especially the upland portions on the western side of this property which contain valuable habitats for listed species.

Florida's population in 2014 is just over 19.5 million persons and demographers project a 2060 population of 36 million or almost double the 2014 population. This growth will be accommodated by a projected loss of 7 million acres of undeveloped lands by 2060 including 2.7 million acres of agricultural lands and one million acres of native Florida habitat. And although Fisheating Creek is located in one of the last sparsely populated areas of Florida, it is also flanked by the southeast and southwest coasts of Florida where a population of almost 7 million people currently reside within less than a two hour drive to the creek. These coastal areas are almost built out and development pressures are increasing toward the inland areas of Florida including Florida's Final Frontier and Fisheating Creek.

Florida demographers predict that Glades County, where most of the Fisheating Creek Ecosystem is located, will be one of three counties that will experience the greatest transformation over the next fifty years as it goes from largely rural to largely urban. In fact, growth pressures are

148

already beginning to be felt in Glades and southern Highlands County as well as other portions of the Last Frontier.

Glades County will undoubtedly grow in the future and the residents there deserve to have a healthy robust economy just as the more populous areas in the State have enjoyed for many years. The county is included with other South/Central Florida Counties in an area designated for participation in the Rural Economic Development Initiative. The intent of this initiative is to encourage and facilitate the location and expansion of major economic development projects of significant scale in such rural communities and also allows the Governor to waive criteria, requirements, or similar provisions of any economic development incentive. And Glades County should consider the Lykes previously stated desire to submit an application to DCA for the Rural Lands Stewardship program so growth can be concentrated in nodes while other larger areas remain in agriculture or natural habitats.

Hopefully Glades County can strike a balance between economic development and preservation of the Fisheating Creek Ecosystem. The county is already ahead of the game due to the designation of the Fisheating Creek Ecosystem, the existence of approximately 68,174 acres of protected lands within the Ecosystem, and the apparent willingness of Lykes to consider selling additional conservation easements within the Ecosystem. All of the remaining lands in need of protection within the Fisheating Creek Ecosystem are owned by Lykes. In order to diversify to compete in today's economy, Lykes has begun to shift the focus of their lands in Glades and Highlands Counties from strictly agriculture to development as well. However, the fact that Lykes owns most of the remaining undeveloped land within Glades County and all of the remaining unprotected land within the Fisheating Creek Ecosystem may be advantageous in achieving a long range plan for Glades County which will accommodate Lykes plans to develop part of their land and preserve and other large scale areas through the RLS program. This would also allow preserved lands to remain in private ownership thereby continuing to contribute to the local economy and provide employment.

The FEGN has identified lands important for creating a statewide ecological greenway network which includes the Fisheating Creek Ecosystem. A critical segment or linkage within this greenway is the Big Cypress-Fisheating Creek Critical Linkage and it has a highest priority ranking because it is considered one of the three most important linkages in the State of Florida.

The future of Florida Forever, Florida's conservation land acquisition program, is uncertain due to Florida's recent budget constraints caused by the economic crisis and funding was not approved for the 2009 and 2011 fiscal years. Fortunately, funding was approved for the 2010 and 2012 fiscal years although at a reduced rate. Even if funding is restored for Florida Forever, there will never be enough money to protect all of Florida's critical lands and waters through fee simple acquisition. More emphasis should be placed on the more economical acquisition of conservation easements and on incentive-based approaches to protect critical lands owned and managed by private individuals.

The Florida Forever Program should consider inclusion of additional lands within the Fisheating Creek Ecosystem as identified by the GAPS report. Those lands are located south of S.R. 74 and U.S. 27 and referred to as the "Ortona/Citrus Center/Hall City" area containing approximately 56,000 acres as well as the area referred to as "Jack's Branch and Bee Branch" containing approximately 36,000 acres.

Within Highlands County, protection of the headwaters areas of Fisheating Creek is also necessary. The recent announcement that the United States Department of Agriculture purchased 26,000 acres of conservation easements in Highlands County adjacent to Fisheating Creek which will include wetland restoration is a good first step and restoration will undoubtedly improve water quality in the creek as well. Hopefully additional lands can be preserved within the headwaters of the creek. If Bluehead Ranch is developed in the future, approval of permits must be contingent on assurances that the water quality of Fisheating Creek will be protected. This goes for any other future developments proposed within the drainage area of Fisheating Creek such as Westby Ranch which has not yet been approved.

One of the keys to preserving the natural resources in the Final Frontier as well as the remaining unprotected lands in the Fisheating Creek Ecosystem is preservation of the existing cattle ranches. Cattle ranches represent some of the most important remaining parcels of contiguous native habitat in the State. These ranches conserve the region's biodiversity necessary for many of Florida's remaining threatened and endangered species. In addition, Central Florida's low intensity cattle ranches provide not only cow calf production but ecosystem services which complement and preserve their natural systems. Cattle ranches are also important to the economy in Florida contributing $348 million to the economy in 2003. The proportion of total revenue contributed to the tax base, although small, is more than enough to pay for what little services ranches require from local governments. The State must try to provide economic incentives to ranchers which will keep up with escalating land values in order to compete with the developers money and encourage ranchers to stay in the business.

With the combined efforts of local, State and Federal governments, environmental organizations, citizens and land owners, more land within the Final Frontier and Fisheating Creek can be protected so that Floridians living in 2060 can look back at our generation and say that we Floridians had the forethought and wisdom and selflessness to preserve these areas for everyone to enjoy forever.

BIBLIOGRAPHY

Belden, Robert C.; McBride, Roy T. *Florida panther Peripheral Areas Survey - Final Report* (Florida Game and Freshwater Fish Commission - August 2, 2006)

Maehr, David S. *The Florida panther - Life and Death of a Vanishing Carnivore* (Island Press, Washington, D.C. - 1997)

Thatcher, Cindy A.; van Manen, Frank T.; Clark, Joseph D. *An Assessment of Habitat North of the Caloosahatchee River for Florida panthers* (Final Report to FWS - June 30, 2006)

U.S. Fish and Wildlife Service *Florida panther Recovery Plan* (Third Revision - November 1, 2008)

Millsap, Brian A. *Summer Concentrations of American Swallow-Tailed Kites at Lake Okeechobee, Florida, With Comments on Post Breeding-Movements* (Florida Field Naturalist, November 1997)

Meyer, Kenneth D.; Zimmerman, Gina M. *Threats and Potential Management at The Pre-Migration Roost of Swallow-tailed Kites on the Fisheating Creek Wildlife Management Area* (Florida Game and Freshwater Fish Commission - June 2, 2007)

Meyer, Kenneth D. *Conservation and Management of The Swallow-tailed Kite* (Florida Game and Freshwater Fish Commission - December, 2004)

A Conceptual Management Plan for Fisheating Creek Wildlife Management Area 2003-2008 (Florida Game and Freshwater Fish Commission - February 2003)

Recreation Master Plan for Fisheating Creek Wildlife Management Area (Florida Game and Freshwater Fish Commission - January 2005)

Guide To The Natural Communities Of Florida (Florida Natural Areas Inventory - February 1990 and June 2009 Draft Update) Cox, James; Kautz, Randy; MacLaughlin, Maureen; Gilbert, Terry

Closing The Gaps In Florida's Wildlife Habitat Conservation System (Florida Game and Freshwater Fish Commission, Office of Environmental Services - February 1994)

Endries, Mark; Stys, Beth; Mohr, Gary; Kratimenos, Georgia; Langley, Susan; Root, Karen; Kautz, Randy Wildlife Habitat Conservation Needs in *Florida - Updated Recommendations for Strategic Habitat Conservation Areas (*Florida Fish and Wildlife Conservation Commission, Office of Environmental Services - February 2009)

Nicodemus Slough/C-19 Project - Conceptual Design Report July 1986, (South Florida Water Management District)

Lake Okeechobee Watershed Construction Project - Phase II Technical Plan - (South Florida Water Management District - February 2008)

Williams, Lovett; Austin, David; Peoples, Tommie *Turkey Harvest Patterns On A Heavily Hunted Area* - (Florida Game and Freshwater Fish Commission - 1974)

Austin, David *Trapping Turkeys In Florida With The Cannon Net* - (Florida Game and Freshwater Fish Commission - 1965)

Parsons, Ross *Lykes Fisheating Creek Wildlife Management Area* - (Florida Wildlife Magazine - 1974)

Delaney, Michael F, et al *Florida Grasshopper Sparrow Distribution, Abundance, and Habitat Availability - (*Southeastern Naturalist - 2007)

Delaney, Michael F.; Cox, Jeffery A. *Florida Grasshopper Sparrow Breeding, Distribution and Abundance in 1984* - (Florida Field Naturalist - 1986)

Delaney, Michael F.; Linda, Stephen B. *Characteristics of Abandoned and Occupied Florida Grasshopper Sparrow Territories* - (Florida Field Naturalist - 1994)

Shriver, Gregory W.; Vickery, Peter V. *Aerial Assessment of Potential Florida Grasshopper Sparrow Habitat: Conservation in A Fragmented Landscape* (Florida Ornithological Society - February 1999)

U.S. Fish and Wildlife Service *Multi-Species Recovery Plan For South Florida* (May 18, 1999)

Bielefeld, Ron; *Florida mottled duck Telemetry Annual Report 2009* (Florida Fish and Wildlife Conservation Commission - August 10, 2009)

Johnson, Fred A.; Montalbano, Frank; Hines, Tommy C.; *Population Dynamics and Status of the Mottled Duck on Florida* (Florida Game and Fresh Water Fish Commission, 1984)

Stys, Beth; *Ecology of the Florida Sandhill Crane* (Florida Game and Fresh Water Fish Commission, July 1997)

Williams, Lovett E.; Phillips, Robert W.; *Capturing Sandhill Cranes With Alpha-Chloralose* (Journal of Wildlife Management 1997)

Williams, Lovett E.; Nesbitt, Stephen A.; *A Trial Translocation of Sandhill Cranes* (Florida Game and Fresh Water Fish Commission, 1973)

Preble, George Henry; *A Canoe Expedition Into The Everglades in 1842* (United Service Journal, A Quarterly Review of Military and Naval Affairs, 1883)

Dixon, Jeremy Douglas; *Conservation Genetics of the Florida black bear* (U. of F. Masters Thesis, 2004)

Maehr, David S., University of Kentucky, et al; *Status of the black bear in South-Central Florida* (Florida Field Naturalist - 2004)

Eason, Thomas H., Ph.D.; *Conservation Strategy for the black bear in Florida* (Florida Fish and Wildlife Conservation Commission - July 2003)

Maehr, David S. et al, Florida Game and Freshwater Fish Commission; *Long Distance Movements of a Florida black bear* (Florida Field Naturalist - February 1988)

Hoctor, Tom; *Update of the Florida Ecological Greenways Network* (U. of F. GeoPlan Center for DEP - June 2004)

Hoctor, Tom; Wood, Jim; *Identification of Critical Links Within the Florida Ecological Greenways Network* (U. of F. GeoPlan Center for DEP - July 2002)

Hoctor, Tom, et. al.; *Land Corridors in the Southeast: Connectivity to Protect Biodiversity and Ecosystem Services (March 21, 2007)*

Brown, Mary E.; *Investigation of a Synergistic Relationship Between Conservation and Cattle Ranching: A GIS Modeling Analysis in South Central Florida.* (U. of F. Masters Thesis, 2008)

Hermanson, Betsey: *Florida Ranchlands - Areas of Conservation Value and Opportunities for Restoration* (U.C.F., The Palmetto - Fall 2007)

Bohlen, Patrick J.; Swain, Hilary M. *Ranching for Environmental Services: Public Benefits From Private Lands* (MacArthur Agro-ecology Research Center and Archibald Biological Station 2007)

Vogel, Mike; *Top 200 Private Companies - Family Feud* (Florida Trend Magazine, September 1, 2001)

Konkoly, Jim; *Lykes Official Blasts Growth-Limit Plans* (Highlands Today, December 25, 2007)

Barnett, Cynthia; *Final Frontier - Growth is Coming to Florida's Heartland. Who Gets to Say Where it Goes and How.* (Florida Trend Magazine - July 1, 2006)

Farr, James A., PhD; Brock, O. Greg, PhD *Florida's Landmark Programs for Conservation and Recreation Land Acquisition.* (Sustain - Journal of Environmental and Sustainability Issues, Kentucky Institute for Environment and Sustainable Development at the University of Louisville - Spring/Summer 2006).

Pinnell, Gary; *Crist Has Red-Lighted Toll Roads; Supporters Say Projects Aren't Stalled* (Highlands Today - June 7, 2007)

Townsend, Billy; *110-Mile Tollway Could Reshape Rural Central Florida* (Tampa Tribune, February 9, 2007)

Metcalf and Eddy for South Florida Water Management District; *Fisheating Creek Sub-Watershed Feasibility Study Phase I, Document and Data Summary Report Final* (March 2009)

Department of Community Affairs; *Objections, Recommendations and Comments Report - Highlands County 10-1ER EAR Based Comprehensive Plan Amendments* (June 10, 2010)

Associated Press; *U.S. pledging $89 million for Everglades land* (July 20, 2010)

Florida Cattleman's Association; *Water Quality Best Management Practices for Cow/Calf Operations in Florida* (June 1999)

Jhang, J. et al for ASAEB Annual Meeting; *Modeling Phosphorous Load Reductions of Agricultural Water Management Practices on a Beef Cattle Ranch* (July 2006)

Capece, John C. et al for Rangeland Ecology and Management 60(1); *Soil Phosphorous, Cattle Stocking Rates, and Water Quality in Subtropical Pastures in Florida, USA (January, 2007)*

Bohlen, Patrick J., Swain, Hilary M.; *Ranching for Environmental Services: Public Benefits from Private Lands* (Abstract - MacArthur Agro-Ecology Research Center and Archbold Biological Station, 2007)

Pandey, Vibhuti; *Analysis and Modeling of Cattle Distribution and Complex Agro-Ecosystems of South Florida* (U. of F. Masters Thesis, 2007)

Secretary of the Interior; *The Impact of Federal Programs on Wetlands* (March , 1994)

USDA, NRCS; Farm Bill 2008 - Wetlands Reserve Program (May, 2008)

Wilson Miller, Inc.; *Blue Head Ranch Sustainable Community Overlay, Environmental Supplement* (Highlands County 2010 EAR-Based Comprehensive Plan Amendments, Data and Analysis March , 2010)

DEP, Division of Water Resource Management; *Water Quality Assessment Report for the Kissimmee River and Fisheating Creek (2006)*

FindLaw (Case Law No. 93-3179); *Lykes Inc. vs. United States Army Corp. of Engineers (September 20, 1995)*

Florida Department of Environmental Protection; *Emergency Final Order - Emergency Authorization for Placement of Flow Blocking Structures in a Newly Opened Navigation Cut in Cowbone Marsh Part of Fisheating Creek Within Glades County* (July 2, 2010)

Enterprise Florida; *Glades County Profile* (2009)

Florida's Heartland Rural Economic Development Initiative; *Glades County Visioning Process - Vision Report* (June 2006)

Board of Trustees of the Internal Improvement Trust Fund of the State of Florida, Save Our Creeks, Inc, Environmental Confederation of Southwest Florida, Inc.; *Settlement Agreement* (May 25, 1999)

156

163Florida Fish and Wildlife Conservation Commission - Office of Recreation Services; *Recreation Master Plan for Platt Branch WEA*

Swain, Hilary: *A Tribute to Mason Smoak and David Maher* - Archbold Biological Station, June 24, 2008)

Sears, William H.: Fort Center - An Archaeological Site in the Lake Okeechobee Basin (1982)

Roadside America.Com; *Gaskins Cypress Knee Museum Closed* (June 2000)

Davis, Marc; *Former local developer has big plans for a Florida ranch* - Virginia-Pilot (December 5, 2007)

Staats, Eric; *Conservation groups call for tripling of Florida panther refuge in eastern Collier County* - NaplesNews.com (August 23, 2010)

mcdanielranch.net *History of McDaniel Ranch* (August 31, 2010)

Stark, Peter; *The Last Empty Places – A Past and Present Journey Through the Blank Spots on the American Map* - (Ballantine Books, 2010)

Cortner, Marvin G.; *Northeast District Would Fuel Jobs* (Osceola News Gazette, April 28, 2010)

Spear, Kevin; *Deseret Ranch Owners Pull Request to Rezone Property* (Orlando Sentinel, July 8, 2008)

Florida Ranchlands Environmental Services Project (www.fresp.org October 20, 2010)

1000 Friends of Florida; *Planning Strategies for the Everglades Agricultural Area* (October 2009)

Quinlan, Paul; *Vast new refuge weighed for northern Everglades* (The Palm Beach Post News, March 3, 2010)

Whirls, Tracy; *Lykes-Duda move forward with intermodel logistics center*

(Glades County EDC Newsletter, March-June, 2010)